OFFICIAL
SCOTLAND
SUPPORTERS' BOOK

THIS IS A CARLTON BOOK

This edition published in 1998

10 9 8 7 6 5 4 3 2 1

A CIP catalogue record for this book is available from the British Library

ISBN hardback 1 85868 499 4
ISBN paperback 1 85868 562 1

Project Editors: Martin Corteel & Roland Hall
Project art direction: Diane Spender
Production: Sarah Schuman
Picture research: Justin Downing
Design: Michael Spender

Author's acknowledgements
I am grateful to Henry Smith for his encouragement, to the *Sunday Times* for its database, and to Susan Stewart for everything. Thanks also to Douglas Alexander, Roddy Forsyth, Kenny MacDonald, Andy Ward, Andy Mitchell and Phil Shaw. This book is for Robert and James Sweeney, comrades in the North Enclosure.

Printed in Italy

All player statistics in this book are correct up to February 28, 1998.
All other statistics and line-ups were correct at the time of going to press.

OFFICIAL
SCOTLAND

THE·SCOTTISH·FOOTBALL
·ASSOCIATION·
®

SUPPORTERS' BOOK

KEVIN McCARRA

CARLTON

Contents

Gordon Strachan puts the pressure on England

The lure of football. A Scotland fan in Latvia, 1996

For the fourth time in a World Cup tournament, Scotland will face Brazil. This chapter examines the form of the Scotland team, as well as Brazil, Norway and Morocco, the other three group opponents.

Relives Scotland's rocky ride to France: from the opening match against Austria in August 1996 to the crucial 2–0 victory over Latvia in October 1997 that confirmed Scotland's place in the 1998 World Cup.

Biographies and fact files on the star players whose skills have inspired a nation.

The full lowdown on Craig Brown, the man who has guided Scotland to the World Cup.

Darren Jackson led the attack in 1997

Introduction

According to the calendar, the World Cup comes around once every four years. In reality, of course, its appearances are not intermittent at all. The thought of it drums away constantly inside the mind of anyone with the slightest care for football.

Separation from the World Cup sharpens the interest. Having failed to qualify for USA 94 four years ago, Scotland have not appeared in the finals since 1990 and the period in exile adds to the savour of the games in France this summer.

The tournament is a culmination. For Craig Brown, the manager, it brings the opportunity to pit his wits against Mario Zagallo, architect of the incomparable Brazil side of 1970 and coach of the present, much-vaunted team. For many of the Scotland players, the 1998 World Cup is the pinnacle of their careers, because they are too old now to hope to play in the competition again. For every member of the squad, it is an escape from the familiarity of domestic football. It can, for good or ill, be very easy in a World Cup to commit an act that is never forgotten.

Supporters, scraping around for funds and hunting for tickets, are urged on by the need to be part of an event that bears no relation to any other series of games. Coach, players and fans are united by the understanding, too, that this year is part of a Scottish entanglement with the World Cup that stretches back almost half a century. When the finals are in prospect, the current squad and the matches it has played must always be reviewed, but the past is not forgotten either.

All the earlier campaigns rush back into the nation's long conversation with itself. To a certain extent, they are pored over in the faint belief that there are lessons to be learned and mistakes to be renounced. Besides that common sense of purpose, there is also a need to steep oneself in the previous passions that have fuelled players and crowds. The World Cup is played on peaks of emotions, and Scotland are still to return to the heights reached in the win over Sweden in Genoa at the 1990 finals.

Colin Hendry and the others are part, too, of another climb that began in the foothills of the 1950s, and which has yet to be completed. It can feel, now and again, as if Scotland's tale of excruciating disappointment has become wearisome, but the desire to smash through the barriers is always fresh and keen. Although the 1998 World Cup makes unprecedented demands on Scotland, with the opening match against Brazil, Brown's experienced players will be finely honed.

In representing the nation, they take the field on behalf of those who have gone before them in the dark blue jerseys. If, after so long a wait, there should be cause for pride this year, the Scotland team will realize not only its own dreams but also those nurtured by generations of their countrymen.

Gary McAllister was vital to Scotland's progress to the World Cup Finals, even though injury prevents him from taking part

Chapter 1
Prospects for France

On every continent great swathes of the population will tune in to the opening game of the World Cup finals and, once their gaze has soaked up the pageant and ceremony that precede the kick-off, their eyes will fall on Scotland. In an existence stretching back to the first international match ever played, against England in Glasgow in 1872, the national team has never experienced a moment of such prominence.

On June 10, at the Stade de France, in the northern suburbs of Paris, Scotland will play Brazil, the World Cup-holders in a game that throws open the doors to the greatest sporting event of all.

Craig Brown's team are conscious of their country's heritage and could never be satisfied with their simple presence in the new 80,000-seater spaceship of an arena. Tradition will insist that Craig Brown's side should believe in its own ability to compete, even against Brazil. Scotland will make history that afternoon, for the match is the 100th, including

Craig Brown's calm and good humour will protect him from the World Cup pressures

qualifiers, that they have played in the World Cup over the past 48 years.

This century of games merits a little celebration, but it might also aggravate a feeling of frustration.

Although this will be Scotland's eighth appearance in the finals themselves, they have never advanced beyond the opening round. Whatever the result, the present-day team must leave the Stade de France with enough morale to fuel a bid to make history. Brown will surely drum into his squad's minds the message that the other two matches in group A, against Norway and Morocco, cannot be allowed to turn into afterthoughts.

If Brazil continue to occupy a prime position in the imagination, it is because they must be faced first. Many teams have struggled over the years because they carry their deep admiration for Brazil on to the field with them. The task for Mario Zagallo's side will be far easier if they find deferential opponents in front of them. Scotland have had a taste of that kind of mood.

In 1982, Scotland fans became starry-eyed about the slick Brazilian goals that were paving the way to a 4–1 defeat for their own team. Brown is obliged to ensure that his players do not enter into a carnival spirit on June 10.

Been there, done that

The manager holds experience in high esteem and there are many mature members of the squad who will refuse to be stagestruck. After the European Championships of 1992 and 1996, Scotland, in any case, are accustomed to the big occasion, even if they have never sampled anything like the opening game of a World Cup. As in 1992 and 1996, he is taking the party to the USA for its preparations.

The players will not be allowed to loll around while recovering from the rigours of the club season. Scotland have settled upon a fairly severe training regime. The exertion in humid conditions at high temperatures ensures increased benefits for the heart and lungs when the team returns to a less extreme climate. The dividends were obvious in the hyper-active performance with which Scotland overwhelmed Switzerland at Euro 96.

Prior to that tournament, during their stay in Connecticut, the team were derided for losing to the USA in a friendly, but the players were still heavy-legged at that stage because of the quantity of stamina work they had completed. The fine tuning comes later.

It would be pleasant if Scotland avoided defeat in their preparatory matches this year, but the same procedures will be followed for the same reasons.

Pride of Scotland

Brown has few selection difficulties. Those with a craving for novelty would appreciate the excitement of major alterations to the line-up, but such a policy makes no sense. If there were better players around, Brown would already have picked them in the qualifying fixtures which ended last autumn. Subtle developments do occur, however, and the manager has sensitive judgements ahead of him, as when choosing between two goalkeepers with superb records, Jim Leighton and Andy Goram.

There are issues to consider in other areas as well, particularly with Matt Elliott giving outstanding displays in central defence for Leicester City. He won his first cap in November 1997, against France, but one can expect to see a great deal more of him in times to

Jim Leighton, at 39, has the experience to issue instructions that defenders will follow

come. His claims to a place are already becoming more marked. Brown is particularly well-served in midfield and there he will probably wish only to detect signs that all remains well with John Collins and Paul Lambert.

The constitution of the attack continues to be the most unpredictable area. The manager knows how limited his resources are in that department, with Kevin Gallacher the only established forward in the squad who is playing regularly for his club team and scoring goals. In consequence, Brown has been studying candidates in Britain and evaluating the possibility of restoring Scott Booth, who was generally a substitute with Borussia Dortmund in the first half of the season, but made a strong early impression at Utrecht after joining them on loan in February.

The definitive answers will be arrived at in the Scottish squad's World Cup base, near Avignon, in the south-east of France. This is to be a competition of journeys, with each nation appearing in three different cities during the group stage. Brown has decided that brief, overnight trips to the relevant venues for each match are preferable to the entire uprooting of the party. He may have given some thought to events at the 1990 World Cup in Italy when the side established itself in Rapallo on the Ligurian coast and ended its stay there after a pugnacious victory over Sweden in Genoa.

Something may have been lost in the relocation to Aosta, in the Alps, that followed, and Scotland went out of the competition after a miserable match with Brazil, and a 1–0 defeat, in Turin. The best result Scotland have ever achieved against Brazil is the 0–0 draw at the 1974 World Cup, and the siting of the training camp will hardly guarantee triumph this year. All the same, a settled home might foster consistency of performance.

Demand exceeds supply

With games spread over almost a fortnight, the players can hardly be confined to barracks at all times, but they will be unable to act as tourists. That privilege belongs to the fans. The SFA travel club, already concerned about the limited quantity of available tickets, closed its doors to new members as soon as Scotland had qualified for the finals. There are around 12,000 people on its books and even if they were the only ones endeavouring to follow the team there would be a mighty presence in France.

BRAZIL

Popularity can be a prison. Brazil have been the best-loved team on the planet for decades, yet that hysterical devotion creates pressures that can warp the people who are at the focus of the frenzy. Having won the World Cup in 1994, it might have been thought that the manager, Carlos Alberto Parreira, would have clung to the post so that he could bask in the adoration and continue to work with wonderful players. Not at all.

"Three years in that job is more than enough for any human being," he said after he had resigned.

It took 24 years, but the World Cup at last returned to Brazilian hands in 1994

This summer, Brazil will have a better squad than any of their rivals in France, but more will be expected of them as well. Should Roberto Carlos be unable, for example, to deliver the sort of curling free-kick that astonished physicists as much as it excited fans when he scored against France in Le Tournoi last year, there will be a sense of anti-climax. Winning matches is only one small part of the demands placed on Brazil and they have not always coped with the expectations.

If the World Cup only existed to discover which nation's players possessed the most skill and imagination, then Brazil might take the trophy into permanent custody. In reality, though, the tournament has often been a torment to them. When Pele and the others collected the World Cup in 1970 nobody would have guessed that another 24 years would be required before Brazil repeated the triumph. On occasions, their own flair seemed to mock them.

Most of the planet went into mourning when the stylish side of 1982 contrived to destroy itself against

Italy. It took Parreira to insist that even Brazilians had to observe the disciplines of the game if they were to succeed. USA 94 is recalled with pleasure because of two excellent forwards, the untamable Romario and the selfless Bebeto, but that pair stand out in the memory because very few other members of the side were allowed the freedom to express themselves.

The majority of the team were cautious and made sure that there was plenty of cover to minimize the possibility of a counter-attack. Only one midfielder scored in the tournament and Rai's goal came from the penalty spot. Rai himself was to be dropped from the Brazil side long before the final as Parreira let everyone see that the pattern he sought to establish mattered more than any individual player. Parreira has a long-standing interest in the precise preparation of players.

World Cup veteran

In 1970, he had been fitness coach to the squad, putting them through a highly-scientific programme that lasted for three months. Mario Zagallo was Brazil's manager that year, just as he is now. Twenty-eight years ago, he, with Parreira's help, took a gloriously gifted group and persuaded them to fit themselves into a framework that put each man's skills to the best use. To add discipline to intuitive talent is an extraordinary feat and it is one that Zagallo will have to repeat this summer.

It is as well that he has winners' medals as a player from the World Cups of 1958 and 1962 because he will need all the know-how he can muster. Zagallo possesses a pool that contains far more creativity than the squad of 1994, and therein lies the problem. Who will attend to the mundane duties of a match? How can such unusual pieces be made to interlock? On the face of it, Zagallo has had few problems with the jigsaw puzzle. The Brazilian Football Federation considered the defeat by Norway last summer to be their first in full international matches since the 1994 World Cup.

Friendlies, however, are sent to mislead a manager. Only this year's tournament in France will establish Brazil's real value. There is eagerness to see the side in such a context. In particular, people will gather to witness Ronaldo play in his first World Cup. In a typical gesture of denial, Parreira never allowed him to come on as a substitute in 1994. There will be no holding him back this year. At 21, he has already collected

Ronaldo's aplomb has scared defences and brought him the comfort of immense wealth

FIFA's Player of the Year award twice.

Since coming to Europe he has played for PSV Eindhoven and Barcelona, and the transfer fee for his move to Inter Milan was £19.8 million. His wages from the Italian club are stated to be £3.5 million a year and his income is topped up by the kind of sponsorship deal that brings in £1 million a year from a sportswear company. There is a certain vulgarity to such sheer quantities of cash, but there are no indications that wealth has damaged his love of the game.

Ronaldo is starting to show that he possesses more than individualism. In January, he was responsible for Inter's 1–0 win over Juventus. The striker was muscular enough to hold off Paolo Montero and quick enough to elude Mark Iuliano, but the surprise came in the beautifully weighted cross that Youri Djorkaeff drove home.

For all that, Ronaldo is a young man and Zagallo seems to fret about the effects of this high-powered career. The manager has different reasons to feel troubled about other players. Romario has been in dispute with his club, Valencia, and relationships with Zagallo have not always been harmonious either. It does look as if the manager possesses riches when one considers that Edmundo delivers goals at the same rate as Ronaldo. Unfortunately, the striker collects red cards with as great an alacrity and was sent off seven times last year.

Whoever is fielded in attack for Brazil should not run short of service. Recent chatter has all concerned the 20-year-old Denilson, who will eclipse Ronaldo's transfer fee when he leaves São Paulo to join Real Betis in Spain for £21 million after the World Cup finals. The price is ridiculous, but he does flay defences with his pace on the wing and his delicate left foot ensures there is subtlety as well as speed. Denilson has also been acquiring goals for his country with some regularity.

The composition of Group A at the World Cup finals was met with glee by the Brazilian public. Given their country's record, high confidence about those matches is pardonable. When you talk to any follower of the team, however, you soon reach the reservations that lie just below the surface of the exuberance. Mention Denilson, for example, and you will hear fans fret that neither he nor Roberto Carlos will do enough defending on the left flank. It is always the same with Brazil. The hopes are entwined with the fears.

NORWAY

Egil Olsen is a shrewd opponent. Bad enough if you must deal with his Norway side in a football match, but worse still if you have to play poker with the manager.

Egil Olsen's sharp mind has given Norway a cutting edge in the 1990s

As Erik Pedersen, the Dundee United midfielder who used to be in the international side, said, "It's not funny at all. He knows what cards you have." With his calculating machine of a brain, Olsen could probably have made his living as a gambler, but his mind has been put to more orthodox uses.

He has announced that he will give up the Norway job after the World Cup. The multiple opportunities then open to him would include an increase in his duties at Oslo's University of Sports and Physical Education, where he is a professor. Olsen reckons that he spends 20 per cent of his time lecturing there at the moment. This is a man who is far removed from the stereotype of a manager and there are several respects in which he is a non-conformist.

Those who attended the World Cup draw in Marseille can testify that he is not ostentatious. Others might flaunt the tailoring of their suits, but he was casually dressed and carrying a carrier bag. Olsen is different.

In the years when British clubs were in awe of continental systems and dreamed of introducing a *libero* to every team, he caused consternation by arguing that the traditional values of British football were still preferable.

He rather proved the point by using those methods against England themselves and seizing the victory, in 1993, which turned out to be the fatal blow to Graham Taylor's hopes of qualifying for the 1994 World Cup finals. Olsen resembles Jack Charlton in outlook, believing that the ball should be played into space rather than delivered to feet. When the system is used properly, it can whip up a great momentum. A lot of disapproval is a common side effect.

Shorn as it is of decoration, the style can be ugly. Gunnar Halle, the defender, believes that Norway get the ball forward more quickly than even his Leeds United team does.

A point to prove

In the coaching world, Olsen's ideas have been met with a lingering antagonism and when Norway had a wretched time at the 1994 World Cup there was a great deal of smug satisfaction. As it turned out, his enemies had not seen the last of the manager or his side. All things considered, Olsen has no reason to apologize.

He has been in charge of the team since 1990 and in those eight years they have averaged only one defeat in every five games. Olsen has proved himself continually, ever since the early days when he took Lyn Oslo to promotion from Norway's Third Division.

The national team's qualification for the 1998 World Cup finals, from a comparatively easy group, did not make much impact, but a 4–2 victory over Brazil in a friendly last summer ensured that Norway were the centre of attention once more.

In that match, Tore Andre Flo scored one of the goals with a move constructed from 13 passes, proof that Olsen's side are capable of elaboration if it suits their purpose. Despite his gangling height, Flo is showing, with Chelsea, that his real *forte* is concise finishing when the ball is on the ground.

The export of Norwegians to English football has reached record levels and, at the beginning of this year, there were 27 of them on the books of British clubs. No wonder Olsen chose to hold January's squad gathering in Blackburn. Although Norway will always be indebted to him, Olsen has been assisted of late by valuable newcomers, such as Manchester United's Ole Gunnar Solskjaer, who make the team less predictable. Thought-provoking though the manager's views may be, it is the players who pose the real threat to Scotland.

MOROCCO

The inclusion of Morocco in their group did not make Scotland fearful, but it left Brown pensive. While Brazil are famed throughout the world and Norwegian footballers are regular visitors to our Saturday night television screens in the coverage of English League matches, Morocco are rather more of a mystery. For Scotland, so adept at dealing with the styles adopted by European nations, they will present a different sort of conundrum.

The analysis of Morocco will be lengthy and neither side will have been able to preserve any secrets by the time they face one another on June 23 in Saint-Etienne. Both countries will then have been on full display in their first two group matches.

Morocco are not novices and it is often forgotten that they finished above England in the group stage of the 1986 World Cup finals. They were also present in the 1994 tournament, even if they were in less noteworthy form on that occasion.

Stars in the making

Morocco might even have been the hosts of the World Cup this year, had King Hassan II been able to persuade FIFA. In any case, France will be congenial soil, given its large Moroccan community. Some believe that 20,000 of their countrymen will attend each of their team's matches. The defensive anchor of the side, Noureddine Naybet, was actually born in the

Salaheddine Bassir has been the spearhead for Morocco since Henri Michel became manager

Moselle region and turned down an invitation to be capped for France at under-21 level.

Naybet has been joined at Deportivo La Coruña by Morocco's most impressive striker, Salaheddine Bassir. Indeed, many others in the squad are to be found at clubs in Spain or Portugal. Bassir is a comparatively recent arrival in Europe but he is well known for the 10 goals, in 16 matches, that steered his country to the finals of both the World Cup and the African Nations Cup this year. Morocco have players of repute in all departments and Mustapha Hadji, also of Deportivo, is viewed as a particularly graceful midfielder.

Morocco ought to receive shrewd guidance in the 1998 World Cup since they are in the hands of the crafty Henri Michel, a former manager of France.

The present Morocco side is very much his own creation and bears little resemblance to the one that could not win a game at USA 94. He will be taking a sound squad to this year's finals.

THE BEST OF THE REST

Hosts under pressure

Hosts can find it hard to enjoy their own party when there is so much to worry about. The same syndrome applies to football tournaments. Precisely because they are playing in their own land, France could easily become fretful.

Fourteen years ago, the national team did keep its nerve to win the final of the European Championship in Paris, but the current side may not have the flair that allowed Michel Platini and the rest to break any *impasse* they encountered in 1984.

There are good players on the present-day scene. France has provided Italy's Serie A with many of its stars, including Marcel Desailly and Zinedine Zidane, while its clubs, despite the transfers, remain potent in European competition. To reduce the sort of pressure exerted on hosts by an excited and nervous population, however, France will need to score freely.

Zinedine Zidane, of Juventus, has joined the elite band of cosmopolitan footballers

Aimé Jacquet, the coach, has still to find the right forwards and, in the 2–1 win over Scotland in November, his attack was made up of Lilian Laslandes, who had never been capped, and Stephane Guivarc'h, who was making his second appearance. The search for a successor to Jean-Pierre Papin continues.

England expects...

Jacquet will not be the only person at the World Cup who wishes he could borrow one or two of England's surplus strikers. Glenn Hoddle, who took over the post from Terry Venables in 1996, may be the right man for the England job, but he has also arrived at the right time.

England probably possesses its best generation of players since Sir Alf Ramsey was choosing the mighty squad that went to the 1970 finals. The profusion of forwards is one sign of the resources. When Alan Shearer returned from injury in January, Hoddle could pencil in the Newcastle United man's name, as well as those of Teddy Sheringham and Robbie Fowler, while reflecting on the claims of Michael Owen, Andy Cole, Les Ferdinand and others.

If everyone is fit, the manager will benefit from a fine balance. David Seaman, Tony Adams and Paul Gascoigne are all still prominent, but they can be complemented with the band of youngsters that includes Paul Scholes, David Beckham and Rio Ferdinand.

Cream of Europe

Should England reach the latter stages of the World Cup, they will hope not to be met there by the indomitable Germany, their conquerors in the 1990 World Cup and Euro 96. Winning the European Championship two years ago must have come as a relief to Berti Vogts, for a German coach without a major trophy is in danger of becoming a pariah. Craig Brown admires Germany above any other nation because they marry great ability with a relentlessly competitive spirit.

Vogts has been partially successful in introducing younger talents, such as Borussia Dortmund's Jorg Heinrich, and Oliver Bierhoff has flourished in the past two years, but hopes will still rest on Jurgen Köhler, Matthias Sammer, Andy Möller and, perhaps, Jürgen Klinsmann. They will have to prove that they are fit enough and eager enough to succeed once again.

Tradition is a mighty force that courses through not only Germany, but also Italy. The two countries have each won the World Cup on three occasions. Of late, Italy and their coach, Cesare Maldini, have come in for much criticism. Having failed to defeat England in Rome, the national team had to tolerate the indignity and unease of a two-leg play-off with Russia before they could take their place in France. Maldini's reputation suffered in the process. It would be foolish, all the same, to think that an accomplished squad, which includes his son Paolo, the great AC Milan full-back, will not be put to good use in France.

History suggests that the European nations will enjoy an advantage on their own continent and Brown has a suspicion that the beneficiaries will include Romania. Those who remember their unhappy experiences at Euro 96 might be tempted to ridicule the thought of them as contenders. In England there was a suspicion that Anghel Iordanescu's squad was a doddery bunch who were heading only for retirement. The World Cup qualifiers, however, brought rejuvenation.

They won nine of those ten matches and drew the other, scoring 37 goals and conceding four. When the mood in the camp is right, Gheorghe Hagi, Dan Petrescu, Gheorghe Popescu and all the other well-established faces still constitute a potent team. England ought to be wary in Group G of the World Cup. Romania and other European nations occupied seven of the quarter-final places when the tournament was played in 1994, and it will be difficult for other countries, with the obvious exception of Brazil, to break the cartel this summer.

African champions?

Nigeria are engaged in tapping their potential. Having won the Olympic title in Atlanta, they will be billed as the nation most likely to bring the World Cup trophy to Africa.

The talent of players like Jay Jay Okocha and Sunday Oliseh is constant, but a whirl of change always seems to be whipping through the organization of Nigerian football. In their new manager, they may just have found the right man to prepare the side. Bora Milutinovic, a Serb, has demonstrated his worth with many other countries. Hard though they may try, Scots will never be able to forget one particular result he achieved with Costa Rica in 1990.

The Venues

The Stade de France at St Denis, just outside of Paris, is the only newly-built venue for the 1998 World Cup, but the other grounds have all received extensive renovations. The Stade de France saw its first international match on January 28 this year, and will host not only the opening game, but also the Final and other games in between.

The inaugural match in the Stade de France was a 1–0 victory for France over Spain

After the encounter with Brazil in Paris, Scottish fans move to Bordeaux in the south-west of France for the June 16 match with Norway in the 36,500 capacity Parc Lescure.

Some intrepid supporters saw the work-in-progress at Saint-Etienne's Stade Geoffroy Guichard while attending Scotland's game with France there last year. The full capacity will be available when Brown's team returns for the concluding match in the group, against Morocco on June 23. This ground may be unique in world football for being named after a grocer, who started a business that now comprises some 2000 outlets.

It was the sort of information that Scotland came across while conducting their charm offensive in Saint-Etienne before the friendly in November. Pennants, badges and team photos were all distributed, and the industry seems to have been rewarded now that the luck of the draw has sent Brown's team back there.

The locals may feel a degree of goodwill, but genuine enthusiasm for Scotland will depend on the standard and the excitement of the football produced in a series of matches that begins with that contest against the most powerful nation of all.

Chapter 2
The Route to France

If an international match, especially a qualifier for a major tournament, goes badly, weeks or even months might pass before another game brings the chance to wipe out the memory. Similarly, after the exultation of victory, there is no immediate use to which the newly-acquired confidence can be put. The time scale of international football creates a gradually developing drama and an incessant challenge to the men involved.

Craig Brown, like all managers of national teams, has to combine months of careful planning with bursts of improvization when the whole strategy is thrown into confusion by some random occurrence.

For example, from first match to last, it took Scotland 14 months to make their way through to the finals of the 1998 World Cup in France. It was long enough for players to flourish or to fade, to persist or to fall out of contention and even, in the sad case of the injured Paul McStay last year, to retire completely.

Paul McStay's efforts to help Scotland reach France were among the last acts of a fine career

The 14-month campaign to reach the World Cup finals was over. Scotland celebrate after beating Latvia

Scotland have reached the World Cup finals because everyone involved remained thoughtful and adaptable in the face of the varied demands that confronted them. Sometimes, as in Minsk, a defence had to be cobbled together when most of its usual members were unavailable.

Going on instinct

In other cases, Brown needed to trust his instincts, just as he did with the inspired hunch that the veteran John McGinlay should be reinstated for the game with Sweden.

Over the months, there were gratifying surprises as well as nasty shocks. The manager would not claim to have been responsible, just when Scotland needed it most, for the sudden emergence of Kevin Gallacher as a goalscorer of searing incisiveness. If the creation of goals is mysterious, the stopping of them is sheer hard work and the national team's success stemmed from the tightly-knit industry of a well-drilled ensemble.

Brown had instilled that unity and it remained in evidence throughout the exultation, anxiety and infrequent despondency of the campaign. Although the preparations to deal with each set of opponents were impeccable, tactics are only effective when the players are eager to bring them to life. Scotland had fallen short in the bid to reach the 1994 World Cup in the USA and that disappointment was instructive. The squad seemed resolved that they would not let another opportunity slip away.

There might have been a little difficulty with the lighting on one famous occasion, but Scotland's dream was never to be plunged into darkness.

AUSTRIA vs. SCOTLAND
A promising start
August 31, 1996 (Vienna)

Football matches exhaust the emotions of the players as much as their muscles. When Scotland produced a barnstorming performance to beat Switzerland 1–0 in their final group match at Euro 96, the intensity of the pride and frustration took its toll on everyone who was there. Despite the victory, a place in the quarter-finals was snatched from Craig Brown's side when Holland rescued themselves with a crucial goal in a 4–1 drubbing by England. For the Scotland squad, indeed the whole nation, the praise was almost insufferable because it was mingled with commiserations.

Down the years and across the major tournaments, the national team has heard too many expressions of sympathy. You could only wonder how this group of players would respond to experiences that had tantalized and tormented them. Had any of them been burnt-out by their latest encounter with adversity?

Duncan Ferguson was part of the confident side that took a point in Vienna

| AUSTRIA 0 |
| SCOTLAND 0 |

Austria:
Konsel, Schottel, Feiersinger, Pfeffer, Schopp, Heraf, Herzog, Kuhbauer, Marasek, Polster (Sabitzer 67), Ramusch (Ogris 76).

Scotland:
Goram, Calderwood, Hendry, Boyd, Burley, G. McAllister, McCall, Collins, T. McKinlay, McCoist (Durie 75), D. Ferguson.

Referee:
M. Piraux (Belgium).

There were fears that they were in no condition to be pitched straight back into further struggles. Scotland's progress through all the qualifiers for the 1998 World Cup that followed was to demonstrate a determination and discipline that delighted supporters but also took them by surprise.

The chance for the team to put behind it that poignant, unavailing win over Switzerland at Villa Park came in Vienna. Brown would not permit himself to be forced into experiments conducted out of panic. He was confident that the men who had served him well were not about to succumb to battle fatigue and his team to face Austria was built along familiar lines. A place was found for Duncan Ferguson, but he was scarcely a newcomer and had only missed Euro 96 through injury. If Brown knew what to expect from his own side, it was far more difficult to guess how strong Austria might prove.

They had not even been present at Euro 96, and the Scotland manager found comfort in the 5–3 defeat by Northern Ireland at Windsor Park that had been the ruin of Austria's hopes. Nonetheless, there was also some ominous evidence about Herbert Prohaska's team. Respect was due thanks to a pair of victories over the Republic of Ireland in that attempt to qualify for the European Championship finals. Austrian footballers had begun to impose themselves on the world at large, and not only when they were clad in their nation's colours.

Some had already made a lucrative move to other countries, with Germany's Bundesliga a particularly common destination, and the process is still continuing. Michael Konsel, the goalkeeper who was then with

Rapid Vienna, has been impressing Italian crowds with his undemonstrative, commanding displays since signing for AS Roma in 1997. As Scotland prepared for the tie, Brown was conscious of the general upsurge of the sport in Austria. Konsel had been between the posts in a Rapid side that, three months earlier, had appeared in the 1996 Cup-Winners' Cup Final, losing only 1–0 to Paris Saint-Germain.

Good away point

Scotland could hear the revival for themselves when they strode on to the field at the Ernst Happel stadium. A crowd of 29,500 did not create congestion on the vast expanses of the ground, but such an attendance amounted to an outbreak of enthusiasm in a country that can be apathetic about its football. Scotland were to prove adept at dousing any excitement before it could begin to inflame the audience. Brown's side found it easy to slip back into established procedures and even the defending, although conducted with efficiency, never had to be sustained for long.

Toni Polster, the Köln forward, had already equalled the record of 34 goals for Austria established by Hans Krankl, but he was not to set a new benchmark against Scotland. Having failed to disturb Colin Calderwood and Colin Hendry, let alone test Andy Goram, Polster was replaced after 67 minutes.

Eventually, Austria, out of necessity, impelled themselves into purposeful attacking, but it was the visitors who could sigh over more missed opportunities than their hosts. In the first half, a shot by Ally McCoist had fizzed past a post and, in the closing moments, Duncan Ferguson climbed well, but put a looping header over the bar.

Having come to Vienna with a minor case of concern about their prospects, Scotland left with a trace of disappointment that they had not scored. Greater penetration on the flanks and a piercing final pass would have brought a goal, because Austria's defence had never governed proceedings.

Brown was content with a conservative approach. Four years earlier, when he was still assistant to Andy Roxburgh, Scotland had made a wretched start to the qualifiers for the 1994 World Cup by playing with ill-advised gusto and losing in Switzerland. The error had not been repeated this time around.

Brown was particularly pleased with Stuart McCall, of Rangers, who had cut off the lines of supply to Austria's attack. "I don't think I have ever seen a better midfield holding performance," the manager said. In addition to a point from their first match, Scotland took home with them the reassuring knowledge that their spirit remained intact.

Colin Hendry comes out on top, climbing above Sabitzer and Ogris of Austria

LATVIA vs. SCOTLAND
Three more points
October 5, 1996 (Riga)

As Scotland's plane touched down in Riga, a small fire broke out in the Arrivals Hall. While it was being dealt with, all the passengers were diverted to a drab yard elsewhere in the airport. The Scotland party stood around in the open air, contemplating the

Latvia's Valerijs Ivanovs (left) tries to evade Craig Burley on a profitable night for Scotland in Riga

LATVIA 0
SCOTLAND 2

Latvia:
Karavajevs, Troickis, Stepanovs, Sevlakovs, Bleidelis, Zemilinskis, Astafajevs, Pahars, V. Ivanovs, Babicevs (Stolcers 46), Rimkus.

Scotland:
Goram, Calderwood, Boyd, Whyte, Burley, McCall (Lambert 46), G. McAllister, Collins, T. McKinlay (McNamara 82), Spencer (Dodds 59), Jackson.

Scotland scorers:
Collins 17, Jackson 77

Referee:
J. Ulrich (Czech Republic).

dowdy surroundings and waiting to be reunited with their luggage.

The inconvenience was trivial, but the supposed glamour of international football was impossible to detect. Scotland, however, have never needed to be reminded of life's niggles and nuisances. Craig Brown has frequently claimed that he delays making detailed plans because they will only be disrupted by unruly events.

He is nonchalant about difficulties. Five of his players had dropped out of the squad for the game in Latvia, but Brown shrugged and remarked that Scotland averaged 5.3 withdrawals per international match. The serenity, in this case, may have contained a certain amount of pretence, because four of the absentees were forwards, with Eoin Jess, Duncan Ferguson, Gordon Durie and Ally McCoist all unavailable.

The impact was great since Brown could only choose his pairing in attack from three strikers, John Spencer, Darren Jackson and Billy Dodds, none of whom had ever scored for Scotland. Dodds could afford to take a relaxed view of the statistic since he was still to win his first cap.

Brown regarded Latvia as the most capable of the three former Soviet republics in Scotland's group. The forward Vits Rimkus, for instance, might have been earning his living with Nürnberg, in Germany's third division, but at that stage he had notched six goals in 10 appearances for his country. Latvia had impressed Brown the previous month when their 2–1 defeat by Sweden was attributed, primarily, to a mistake by

Olegs Karavajevs, the goalkeeper. With their team selection restricted, Scotland were even less open to the delusion that they would be able simply to outclass Latvia.

As assignments go, there are very few World Cup ties that can be considered a sinecure. So far as Brown was concerned, the main advantage possessed by Scotland lay in the store of experience that the players had built up. Against Sweden, Latvia had revealed a certain naivety by conceding both goals to near post headers. However, it was to be the wiles of the Scottish midfield that puzzled the opposition and gave Scotland the lead in Riga.

"Latvia are not streetwise," Brown had declared and a free-kick, awarded on the edge of the area after 17 minutes, vindicated his assessment.

Hero at both ends

Stuart McCall touched it to John Collins, who feinted to set Gary McAllister up for a shot, but then wheeled into space himself. The defenders were fatally slow in recognizing the ruse and Collins had enough time to fire vigorously past Karavajevs.

Without Colin Hendry, who was injured, Scotland were not quite so slick in defence and the protection of the lead had its hazardous moments. It was an open match, with both goalkeepers compelled to demonstrate their gifts. In the period following the interval, it looked as if Latvia might equalize, particularly when, in the 71st minute, Mihailis Zemlinskis hit a booming shot that forced Goram to make a marvellous parry. Marians Pahars tried to force home the rebound, but Collins cleared from the goal-line.

Six minutes later, Darren Jackson was to ease Scotland's fears and fulfil his own ambitions by scoring for his country on his 13th international appearance. He ended the drought with the sort of aplomb that made you wonder how it could ever have lasted so long. Winning the ball from a negligent defence, he slipped round an opponent and broke clear before curling a judicious finish into the cŏrner of the net.

"It's such a relief, I just can't put it into words," Jackson was to say later. "We were on the ropes a bit and owe Andy Goram for a couple of incredible saves."

Scotland did not entirely avoid damage in Riga, as

Darren Jackson's first international goal was a delight to the team as it clinched victory over Latvia

Gary McAllister picked up his second booking of the qualifiers. "He got it for saying 'You're joking' to the referee," an incredulous Brown reported. "There was no swearing."

In Estonia, four days later, there was to be much more to concern Scotland than the suspension of their captain.

ESTONIA vs. SCOTLAND
The phantom match
October 9, 1996 (Tallinn)

For some people, Tallinn is a name swathed in mystique. Others, who think of the city only as the capital of a former Soviet republic, might expect it to be as stunted and depressing as the Communist system from which it has only recently broken free.

The Scottish football supporter sees it in an entirely different light. The fans had been to Tallinn before, for a World Cup qualifier in 1993, and regard the place fondly. Cheap beer, which also attracts Finns who travel across from Helsinki on weekend breaks, accounts for part of the appeal, but it is also a beguiling city, with a vibrant population and an ancient heart where the walls of the buildings are as thick as those of a fortress.

The Scotland party, who flew direct from Riga, also considered a journey to Tallinn a congenial trip. Since 1993, a rapport had built up between the two countries. Estonian officials had travelled to Glasgow to extend their knowledge of football administration. Under a scheme set up by UEFA's Eastern European Assistance Bureau to foster the development of the game in the "new" nations, the SFA had sent mini-goalposts for youngsters and all sorts of other equipment and information to Tallinn. There ought to have been an atmosphere of mutual contentment among the Scottish visitors and residents in the city, for while Craig Brown's side was beating Latvia, Estonia were overcoming Belarus 1–0 to record their first victory in a major tournament.

Bonhomie was not to last. On the eve of the game, Scotland trained at the Kadriorg stadium and found

ESTONIA VS. SCOTLAND (ABANDONED)
Scotland:
Goram, McNamara, Boyd, Calderwood, T. McKinlay, Burley, Lambert, Collins, McGinlay, Dodds, Jackson.
No caps were awarded.

that some of the temporary lighting, mounted on lorries, was not elevated high enough above the field. The beams created glare since they shone across the pitch, rather than down upon it. To the Scots, the situation was unsatisfactory and the SFA notified Jean-Marie Gantenbein, the FIFA commissioner for the game, as well as the ruling body itself, that they were concerned. "Our protest was based on a sporting principle," Jim Farry, the SFA chief executive, was to say later. "Our goalkeeper could not see the ball coming in from the left-hand side."

Sepp Blatter, FIFA's general secretary, was contacted in Geneva and the following morning, at around 9 a.m., Estonia and Scotland were informed that the kick-off was to be brought forward from 6.45 p.m. to 3 p.m. so that the game could be played in daylight. The arrangements for any World Cup tie are complex and to change them at short notice ensures upheaval. The SFA, satisfied that conditions for the match would be satisfactory, sent members of staff round Tallinn to notify fans of the alteration and buses were hired to ferry some of them to the ground.

Craig Brown inspects the floodlighting in Tallinn and a gloomy saga begins to develop

The Estonian reaction was markedly different. It was understandable that they should be peeved by the whole affair, but there was incredulity when it emerged that Teitur Thordarson, the Icelandic coach, and his side would not be complying with the FIFA ruling. Estonia had decided to stick to the original schedule. So it was, shortly before 3 p.m., that John Collins, captain in the absence of the suspended McAllister, led out the Scotland team on to a pitch that contained no opponents. "One team in Tallinn," sang the visiting supporters, with commendable accuracy.

In Estonia's absence, Tosh McKinlay hails the fans as Scotland leave the pitch after the token kick-off

Brown had been convinced that Estonia would show up at the very last moment, but he was wrong. Billy Dodds, who ought to have been making his first appearance in the starting line-up for Scotland, kicked-off by knocking the ball to Collins. Miroslav Radoman, the Yugoslav referee, then blew his whistle to signal the end of the action. The scene was preposterous and the outlandish tale commanded attention across the globe that the game itself could never have secured. For those who were in Tallinn, the humour of the afternoon soon petered out, to be replaced by regret that an important sporting occasion had been supplanted by farce. Scotland supporters had also to calculate the cost of a futile trip to Tallinn. At 5.00 p.m. the Estonia team bus drove into the Kadriorg Stadium. Too late.

SCOTLAND vs. SWEDEN
A big step forward
November 10, 1996 (Ibrox, Glasgow)

The Swedish squad that arrived in Scotland must have been bemused by the inflamed environment into which they had stepped. With its reputation as a peace-loving, enlightened society, Sweden is unaccustomed to antagonism from other countries. In Glasgow, however, the reaction suggested that a traditional enemy such as England was in town. The passions had not been aroused by Tommy Svensson's band of players. Outrage had flared in Scottish hearts three days before the game, when FIFA delivered its verdict on events in Tallinn.

In some quarters it had been taken for granted, after Estonia's abrupt refusal to play the fixture, that Scotland would be awarded the three points for the aborted match in Tallinn. Handing Brown's side a victory that they had not been required to earn on the field would, however, have antagonized other members of a hard-fought group. Estonia could simply have been

---

**SCOTLAND 1
SWEDEN 0**

Scotland:
Leighton, Calderwood, Hendry, Boyd, McNamara (Lambert 46), Burley, W. McKinlay, Collins, T. McKinlay, Jackson (Gallacher 78), McGinlay (McCoist 84).

Sweden:
Ravelli, Nilsson, P. Andersson, Bjorklund, Sundgren, Alexandersson (Larsson 68), Zetterberg (A. Andersson 76), Thern, Schwarz, Blomqvist, Dahlin (K. Andersson 16).

Scotland scorer:
McGinlay 8

Referee:
J. Aranda (Spain).

thrown out of the competition, with their results declared null and void, but that would have been a draconian punishment for a nation that is among the novices of the World Cup.

It was ruled that Estonia's match should be replayed and, later, Monaco was specified as the venue. Scots were flabbergasted by the decision, but peeved too by the circumstances that surrounded it. The World Cup organizing committee was responsible for the judgement and its meeting had been chaired by Lennart Johansson, a Swede.

It also emerged that captain Gary McAllister's suspension, which originally applied to the tie in Tallinn, would have to be served against Sweden instead. Fans directed a volley of irate faxes at Johansson. The organizing committee's verdict would almost certainly have been the same even if he had not participated in its deliberations, but such considerations did not appease the crowd at Ibrox.

"My only worry is that we leave those 47,000 people disappointed," Craig Brown said before the game. He knew, too, that the team's best chance of pleasing the supporters lay in detaching itself from the frenzy of the stadium. "As you get older you realise there is no point in being hysterical," the manager observed.

Belligerence would have been ruinous for a Scotland team that was often to find itself outplayed by the opposition. Sweden probably possessed the most accomplished players in the group and their distinction was obvious at Ibrox.

Early goal decides it

The goal with which Scotland acquired the lead early in the game was a fleeting, if admirable, moment of superiority. The move was succinct as Darren Jackson impishly dummied an angled ball from Tom Boyd to leave John McGinlay in the clear. The Bolton Wanderers striker was back in Scotland's plans after an absence of a year and the assurance built up during a productive period at his club was apparent as he eased the ball past goalkeeper Thomas Ravelli. Soon after, Sweden were exasperated when Martin Dahlin was injured and had to be replaced.

John McGinlay relishes his winning goal after his reinstatement for the emotive tie with Sweden

Colin Hendry and Jim Leighton earned this jubilation with the resistance that defied Sweden at Ibrox

Even so, the dose of discouragement proved small and the visitors grew more and more assertive. Without McAllister, Scotland could not establish a bridgehead in midfield and the team had to huddle around the penalty area while Jonas Thern dictated play in the centre of the pitch. The crowd quaked and gasped, but Brown's side, led by Colin Hendry, defended successfully, if desperately, for long spells. As the manager was to point out afterwards, Jim Leighton did not have a save to make until the 67th minute.

The goalkeeper, chosen because Andy Goram was injured, collected his 75th cap. The feat was marked with a commemorative gold medal from the SFA, but he might also have been decorated for the valour he showed at Ibrox.

In the last quarter of the match, Sweden ought to have seized the goals that would have changed the course of the group, but Leighton again and again defied them when every other defender had been left trailing. Svensson's side had lost unluckily to Austria in Stockholm the previous month and they were further impaired by the dejection of their afternoon in Glasgow.

Brown refused to be bashful about a victory that had not been merited. "We will accept a win after we have been the poorer team," he said. "It's not often we get the breaks."

ESTONIA vs. SCOTLAND
Frustration in Monaco
February 11, 1997 (Monaco)

The Scotland fans who travelled to Monaco took a jocular view of the occurrences that had led to the rescheduling of the match with Estonia. Remembering Tallinn, some supporters in the Louis II stadium wore miners' helmets and others sported plastic glasses which had a pencil torch fixed to them. That whimsical disposition did not survive the evening and there were no Scottish smiles to be found when the game was over.

To begin with, there had been the makings of a

Having arrived in expensive Monaco, the fans then had to find the means to afford its prices

ESTONIA 0
SCOTLAND 0

Estonia:
Poom, Kirs, Hohlov-Simson, Lemsalu, U. Rooba, Reim, Leetma (Oper 75), M. Rooba (Pari 67), Alonen, Kristal, Zelinski.

Scotland:
Goram, McNamara (T. McKinlay 75), Calderwood, Hendry, Boyd, McStay (I. Ferguson 63), G. McAllister, Collins, Gallacher, D. Ferguson, McGinlay (McCoist 62).

Referee:
M. Radoman (Yugoslavia).

celebration. Paul McStay appeared to have surmounted his injuries and returned to the international team for his 76th cap. Nobody had an inkling then that a troublesome ankle that had been the subject of several operations would force him to retire in the close season.

A relaxed squad studied the agreeably affluent surroundings. John Collins, who was in his first season with Monaco after moving from Celtic, knew the area well and

must have found it incongruous to be staying in a hotel with the Scotland side when his apartment was only a few hundred yards along the street.

Against Estonia, nobody felt at home. Scotland made a tentative opening and then, after half-an-hour, enjoyed a misleading period when they appeared to have imposed themselves. In one passage of play, Duncan Ferguson and Gary McAllister both had headers cleared off the line before Tom Boyd thrashed the loose ball against the bar. Mart Poom, the Estonia goalkeeper, also made a series of compelling saves and his side possessed a cohesion that might not have been anticipated.

Nine of the Estonian team were from FC Flora. As for the other two, Marek Lemsalu used to play for FC Flora and the sole exception, Liivo Leetma, was substituted by Anders Oper, of FC Flora. After the interval, Scotland, as they attempted to increase the pressure, became too direct, pumping high balls towards

Ferguson that were comfortably dealt with by lofty figures such as Poom and Lemsalu.

Complete disaster averted

They could even have lost in the final seconds had Marko Kristal played an easy pass to the unmarked Indrek Zelinski instead of shooting impulsively. Few Scots were in the frame of mind to count their blessings. Disenchanted fans cheered Estonia from the pitch and rebuked their own side.

"It was embarrassing," said Craig Brown, "the worst performance in my time as manager." The night may also have been a landmark for Duncan Ferguson. He has not played for his country since and went on to inform the SFA that he no longer wishes to be considered for the national team.

His international career has been one of high promise never fulfilled. In seven appearances he failed to score any goals. Brown had more to concern him that night in Monaco than the future of the Everton forward. The result was so poor that Scotland were never again to be masters of their own fate in Group Four.

No problem with lighting, but the game refused to work for Scotland in Monaco

In addition, this goalless draw revived debate about the condition of a side in which eight players were aged 30 or over. The manager had awkward assessments to make. It was up to him to judge whether a drastic revamping of the team was necessary.

Brown concluded that no such steps were required and remained constant in his belief that experienced men are the most likely to flourish in international football. Those who fretted over the issue had forgotten just how great an effort can ensue when a band of veterans, most of whom had never played in the World Cup finals, are making their last bid to appear on the greatest stage of all.

SCOTLAND vs. ESTONIA
Played five, conceded nil
March 29, 1997 (Rugby Park, Kilmarnock)

Football fans are accustomed to pile into buses, cars and trains in all parts of the country to make their way to Scotland's home games. With Hampden out of service while rebuilding continued, though, the national team also had to hit the road for the qualifiers.

Four venues were to be used and the route took them on a tour of the handsomely rebuilt stadiums that are dotted across the land. The fixture with Estonia was the first international to be played at Kilmarnock's Rugby Park since 1910.

The patriotic concern for Craig Brown's team combined with local pride to create a festive atmosphere at the match. The manager also took a relaxed approach. He had allowed Paul Lambert to play for Borussia Dortmund two days' earlier, even though that meant that he had to be rested and would not play against Estonia. John Spencer was even excused service entirely because Queen's Park Rangers had two important games to play. For his part, Brown was pacing the squad's efforts.

There was a double bill of internationals, with an engagement against Austria to follow four days later. The first part of the exercise was dealt with capably. Estonia were as determined as they had been in Monaco and others were beginning to appreciate them, with Mart Poom having signed for Derby County a few days earlier for £500,000.

SCOTLAND 2
ESTONIA 0

Scotland:
Leighton, Burley, Calderwood, Hendry (W. McKinlay 65), Boyd, McStay, G. McAllister, T. McKinlay, Gemmill, Jackson (McGinlay 83), Gallacher.

Estonia:
Poom, Kirs, Hohlov-Simson, Lemsalu, Meet, Reim, Viikmae (Leetma 72), Zelinski (Arbeiter 81), Pari (M. Rooba 54), Kristal, Oper.

Scotland scorers:
(Boyd 25, Meet, o.g., 52)

Referee:
B. Heynemann (Germany).

Gary McAllister dodges Martin Reim and Janek Meet at Rugby Park

Although Scotland had to make do without the artifice of the suspended John Collins, they gradually located paths through the Estonian ranks, with Tosh McKinlay exerting particular influence on the left wing.

Boyd breaks his duck

The visitors were not immediately subdued and Jim Leighton, who would appear in all the remaining qualifiers, had a significant workload. The game began to bend to Scotland's will in the 25th minute when a cross from McKinlay was cleared only as far as Tom Boyd on the right. The defender's drive initiated a mêlée in which Scot Gemmill was close to scoring before Boyd managed to meet a rebound and guide home a header.

The Celtic player's 43rd cap had been accompanied by his first goal for Scotland. Perhaps the effect was invigorating, for Boyd would also hit the bar before the interval. The full-back took a more familar part in the second Scottish goal, swinging in a cross from the left that was disquieting enough to force Janek Meet to head into his own net.

Scotland had been measured, painstakingly making sure of the points and preparing themselves for a challenge from Austria that was expected to be far more taxing. The draw with Estonia had left Scotland with little room for error in any of the contests that remained.

Paul Lambert in typically competitive mood during Scotland's vital 2–0 win against Austria

SCOTLAND vs. AUSTRIA
Second crucial home win
April 2, 1997 (Celtic Park, Glasgow)

With their efforts to reach the 1998 World Cup finals, Scotland not only won matches but also won back the passionate support of the public. The team has always been a matter of interest, but throughout the continent attendances for international football have dwindled as people grow ever more fascinated by the glamorous and deftly-marketed European club competitions which are contested by cosmopolitan sides. It has been Scotland's achievement in the past two years to prove that international football can be just as thrilling.

The audience was to be reminded as well that there is a special satisfaction in success that unites a whole country in joy. The presence of 46,738 people at the victory over Sweden might have been ascribed to the unusual factors applying to that game, but when enthusiasm continues to be demonstrated on that same scale you could only conclude that the nation had become infatuated with the Scotland team once again. A crowd of 43,295 gathered eagerly at Celtic

---

**SCOTLAND 2
AUSTRIA 0**

Scotland:
Leighton, Calderwood, Hendry, Boyd, Burley, Lambert, G. McAllister, Collins, T. McKinlay, Jackson (McGinlay 75), Gallacher (McCoist 85).

Austria:
Konsel, Schottel (Kogler 46), Feiersinger, Pfeffer, Schopp, Heraf, Aigner (Ogris 81), Wetl, Stoger (Vastic 67), Herzog, Polster.

Scotland scorer:
Gallacher 24, 77

Referee:
N. Levnikov (Russia).

Park and Craig Brown's side found itself responsible for a multitude of dreams and demands.

Scotland discharged those duties spectacularly. There was a common view that Brown's men were a well-drilled unit whose careful strategies left no room for panache. As with most cliches, there was a trace of accuracy in the opinion.

The manager is convinced that Scotland can only prosper in international football if the preparations are meticulous. It is true, as well, that the idiosyncratic players with virtuoso abilities are rarely found on the contemporary scene.

With technique and painstaking distribution, John Collins typifies the distinguished Scotland midfield

Even so, the quality of Brown's squad tends to be massively underestimated. The defence is formidable and the midfield polished, ensuring that Scotland only needed to add prowess in attack. The dumbfounded Austrian players were soon able to attest to the effectiveness of the forwards they had faced.

Kevin Gallacher and Darren Jackson were an unlikely combination, since neither man had ever been a prolific international goalscorer. By appearing in international football at all, Jackson, who was 28 when he made his debut for Scotland, had exceeded some people's expectations.

An exhilarated Kevin Gallacher savours the first goal against Austria

Late in his career, he had begun to realize the lengths to which his counterparts at other clubs would go in order to make their mark. As a squad member at Euro 96, Jackson was persuaded of the importance of weight training by John Collins. The forward, who was then with Hibernian, admits to a little embarrassment that he had not previously applied himself to such sessions, but the conversion came in time to have a great effect on his form. "It has made me more robust and given me a yard extra of pace," he said.

Shaken, stirred then downed

Austria were shaken by the pace and power directed at them from all areas of a side that knew a high-tempo style would be most effective. Brown's players also indulged in bouts of rapid, precise passing that took Scotland to levels of accomplishment unreached by the national side for many years. The visitors could find little respite for they were allowed few worthwhile attacks. Their playmaker, Andreas Herzog, hoped to operate just behind the forwards but in that area he was quelled by Lambert, whose worth was climbing with each month he spent at Borussia Dortmund.

There was verve and power about the opening goal, in the middle of the first half. Gallacher dispossessed Wolfgang Feiersinger before releasing Jackson. Michael Konsel made a partial block, but Jackson recovered possession to pull back a low cross that was swept in by Gallacher.

Anxiety over a slender advantage might have grown, but with 13 minutes left, Scotland found the second goal that allowed the remainder of the game to pass in a haze of revelry. Although Gallacher was lucky to receive a deflection, he was merciless in his use of it, bending a thrilling shot round Konsel.

As it turned out in Group Four, the defeat was not to deter Austria, but it did strengthen the faith that the public had in the Scotland side and that the players had in themselves.

SWEDEN vs. SCOTLAND
Scotland run out of steam
April 30, 1997 (Gothenburg)

Sweden were supposed to be disenchanted. Since the great adventure that carried them to third place in the 1994 World Cup, Tommy Svensson's team had become accident-prone. They had failed to qualify for Euro 96 and there were no signs of subsequent improvement.

Undeserved though the results probably were, their bid to reach the 1998 World Cup finals had been seriously hampered by defeats in Vienna and Glasgow. In Gothenburg, Scotland found the locals genuinely disconsolate and pessimistic.

People in the city knew that Sweden had been beaten in all four competitive matches they had played against Scotland over the previous 17 years. Craig Brown, on the other hand, had every reason to feel satisfied.

"We have got to win the midfield battle against Sweden," he said, "and I think we can." Gary McAllister, who would collect his 50th cap in the Ullevi Stadium, appeared likely to bring expertise to bear. With Borussia Dortmund in the European Cup Final, Paul Lambert also carried an enhanced status.

All such considerations were to prove irrelevant, for the match against Sweden took a form that very few people could have envisaged. Svensson's side adopted the direct, physical style that is mistakenly thought of as a British speciality. The merits of the various midfielders could rarely be studied as Sweden bypassed that part of the field and lashed the ball up to forwards who were abetted by quick support from the rest of the team. It was a pattern that Scotland were unable to break.

Colin Calderwood overwhelms Sweden's Martin Dahlin

**SWEDEN 2
SCOTLAND 1**

Sweden:
Ravelli, Sundgren,
P. Andersson, Bjorklund,
Kamark, Thern, Zetterberg,
Schwarz (Mild 12),
A. Andersson, K. Andersson,
Dahlin.

Scotland:
Leighton, Calderwood,
Hendry, Boyd, Burley,
G. McAllister, Lambert,
Collins, T. McKinlay
(Gemmill 67), Jackson
(Durie 66), Gallacher.

Sweden scorer:
K. Andersson 44, 63

Scotland scorer:
Gallacher 83

Referee: P. Collina (Italy).

Wear and tear takes its toll

They looked weary and could not assemble enough passes to give a different character to the tie. In defence, Scotland were strangely unstable and often on the verge of capsizing. The wear and tear of the season had ripped the fabric of the Scotland side. Some men should probably not have taken part at all. Colin Hendry needed a hernia operation, but his eagerness to continue representing club and country saw the centre-half force himself onward. By then, he needed an extensive series of warm-up exercises to reach the suppleness required for a match.

All the same, Sweden had to be praised. Their two strikers, Martin Dahlin and Kennet Andersson, overflowed with zest and skill. Just before the interval, Dahlin made a barging challenge on Hendry to head-flick the ball to Andersson, who found the net with a classic volley. It was the first goal that Jim Leighton had conceded in a competitive international since the 1990 World Cup finals. Another was to follow in the second half, when Andersson worked himself loose the defence and scored with a shot that took a beneficial deflection off Colin Calderwood.

Kevin Gallacher headed in a McAllister corner near the end, but Scotland had been well-beaten and deserved to lose by a larger margin. They remained at the top of the group, but had played more matches than Sweden or Austria. Brown recognized the poverty of Scotland's display, but declined to dwell on it in public, confining his attention to the practicalities.

"If we win our last three games," he said, "the least we can get is the runners-up place."

Disappointment leaves Scotland weary after Sweden's decisive second goal in Gothenburg

---

**BELARUS 0
SCOTLAND 1**

Belarus:
Satsounkevitch, Lavrik, Ostrovski, Iakhimovitch, Gourenko, Dovnar (Belkevitch 53), Romachtchenko, Chtaniouk, Orlovski (Balachov 66), Khlebossolov (V. Makovski 61), Gerasimets.

Scotland:
Leighton, Burley, Dailly, Boyd, Hopkin (Gemmill 68), Jackson (Dodds 87), Lambert, G. McAllister, T. McKinlay (B. McAllister 79), Gallacher, Durie.

Scotland scorer:
G. McAllister, pen., 49

Referee: A. Cakar (Turkey).

BELARUS vs. SCOTLAND

Back on track
June 8, 1997 (Minsk)

Summer is surgery season. Many footballers, after months of relentless action with their clubs, are bound to be injured or in need of operations by the time the domestic programme is over.

With so many games to be shoe-horned into the calendar, Scotland are reconciled to the need to play important fixtures in June. Craig Brown also appreciates that he will have difficulty in fielding a recognizable team on these occasions. Musing on the problems, Brown counted 14 players he might have chosen to pick for the squad who were simply unavailable.

The absentees were spared delays of up to a couple of hours at the airport on arrival at Minsk, during which puzzling forms had to be completed and a mysterious clerical process endured. That emphasis on bureaucracy was presumably a habit that lingered from Belarus's days as part of the old USSR.

Although the country had established its independence, there were many reminders of the Soviet era and a statue of Lenin still remained in one of Minsk's principal squares. However, the capital, with its great expanses of parkland, provided congenial surroundings for the Scotland supporters.

If those travellers had previously known little about Minsk, they were also unclear as to the Scotland side they would be watching. Brown had been forced to reconstruct the team and, lacking Colin Hendry and Colin Calderwood, was particularly anxious to identify candidates for the new defence that had to be concocted at short notice.

Christian Dailly, Brian McAllister and David Weir had all auditioned in two preparatory matches undertaken immediately before the journey to Belarus. In those games, Scotland had been 1–0 beaten by Wales and had recorded an untidy 3–2 win in Malta.

There tends to be a public panic when Scotland

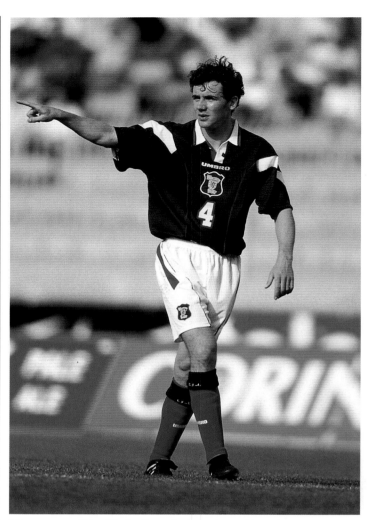

The versatile Christian Dailly has flourished as an international since becoming a centre-half

have poor results in friendlies. "They say that we are in disarray," Brown has remarked wryly of this syndrome. "Why is it always that word 'disarray'?"

As another manager observed, defeat in a friendly can be a good sign if it indicates that genuine experiments have been undertaken. The results matter far less than the quality of the information that has been gleaned. The two games clarified the situation for Brown and he concluded that it would be unwise to employ too many of the newcomers in Belarus.

Shuffling the pack

The manager preferred a reshuffle, with Craig Burley being moved from wing-back to centre-half. Only Dailly, of those tried, played from the start, and he has continued to hold his place in the line-up ever since. His 34 caps at under-21 level are said to be a world

Gary McAllister stayed calm to convert the penalty against Belarus in one of the key matches

record and this versatile player, who has now settled in central defence, is particularly well-suited to the more cultivated requirements of international football.

Alex Ferguson, the Manchester United manager, had been effusive when recommending Dailly to Brown. The 24-year-old's skill allows him to carry the ball forward and forge a valuable link with the midfield. Brown had a good idea of what Dailly might accomplish, but the capacities of Belarus were more difficult to discern.

Rivals in a slump

The 1–0 victory over Holland in a Euro 96 qualifier had established Belarus's credentials and, with 13 of their 19-man squad playing in the Russian League, it was clear that their footballers were well-regarded. On the other hand, recent results had been poor and Mikhail Vergeyenko, in his second spell as manager of the national team, had lost all three matches since being reappointed to the post. He was hardly responsible for the malaise, for Belarus, since that remarkable win over the Dutch in June 1995, had notched a paltry two victories in 17 internationals.

The resolve of Vergeyenko's side to improve that record ensured a disquieting contest for Scotland in Minsk's Dynamo Stadium. A 40-yard drive from Erik Iakhimovitch that hit the bar in the sixth minute constituted the most dramatic danger in the first half, but there were many other moments of alarm. Scotland were shielded by Jim Leighton's alertness and also by the composure of Paul Lambert. The midfielder had won the European Cup with Borussia Dortmund 11 days earlier and a sense of assurance still surrounded him as he methodically restored order around the Scotland penalty area.

The exhaustion of a prolonged season and the humid weather in Minsk drained the side, but the resolve had not diminished. With a piece of alert, shrewd play, Scotland took the lead.

Gathering Gordon Durie's pass, Darren Jackson chose not to shoot, but instead sprinted directly at Iakhimovitch. The defender's hesitancy led to a mistimed tackle that flattened the Hibs forward. Gary McAllister had missed his previous penalty for Scotland, in the 2–0 defeat by England at Euro 96, but the experience had left no residue of doubt. The penalty in Minsk was flighted into the top corner, giving McAllister his first goal for Scotland in five years.

Still Belarus refused to become woebegone. As is their habit, they brought on the thrilling Vladimir Makovski who plays in both under-21 and full international fixtures. With the two games against Scotland taking place on the same weekend, he could make only a limited appearance in each.

The substitute failed to take one opportunity for an equalizer and then created another for Sergei Gerasimets, who dithered and had his shot blocked by Scot Gemmill. Scotland had won the game and those who wondered quite how they had contrived to do so were given their answer by Brown.

"The legs were gone and, in some cases, the brain," he said, "but the heart was huge."

SCOTLAND vs. BELARUS
Almost there
September 7, 1997 (Pittodrie, Aberdeen)

This was the match whose date mattered more to some people than its outcome. It was originally scheduled for September 6, but had it gone ahead as intended it would have taken place on the same day as the funeral of Diana, Princess of Wales.

**SCOTLAND 4
BELARUS 1**

Scotland:
Leighton, Calderwood, Boyd, Dailly, Burley, G. McAllister (Hopkin 50), Lambert, Collins, T. McKinlay, Durie (McCoist 46), Gallacher (Dodds 85).

Belarus:
Shantolosov, Lavrik, Ostrovski, Geraschenko, Dovnar, Gerasimets (Balashov 78), Belkevitch, Jouravel, (Tcherninski 65) Kulchii, Gourenko (Orlovski 52), Katchuro.

Scotland scorers:
Gallacher 6, 57, Hopkin 55,88

Belarus scorer:
Kachuro 65, pen.

Referee:
M. van der Ende (Holland).

The postponement of an international game, with all the logistical problems that then arise, is a major decision and it originally appeared that the fixture would proceed as planned, with everyone at Pittodrie paying their respects to the late Princess in a two-minute silence before kick-off.

After all, no accusations of impropriety had ensued when Sir Winston Churchill's state funeral, on January 30, 1965, had been followed throughout Britain by a full programme of matches. In 1997, however, there were vehement and occasionally hysterical protests over the timing of Scotland's game with Belarus. The

A piper at Pittodrie plays The Flowers of the Forest as a lament for Princess Diana

various governing bodies ultimately agreed that the match should take place a day later than planned, on September 7. And nobody who was present that afternoon will ever forget the austere beauty of the lament The Flowers of the Forest that was played by a lone piper before the match began.

It was almost cruel that the Scotland team, after a week of rancour and debate, should be expected to focus fully on the contest. The players therefore deserve great praise for the purpose and panache they exhibited. The morale of the Belarus squad was assumed to be in disrepair after the long sequence of poor results, but Scotland needed to act quickly to discourage them further. The situation required Brown to draw upon all of his experience because the deployment of his resources was complicated by a variety of factors.

Tosh McKinlay had played in all eight of the World Cup qualifiers, extending an international career that had started belatedly. The left-back had been engaged in building his house when summoned, at short notice during one of the customary injury crises, to join the

Scotland squad for a match with Greece in 1995. McKinlay, who was then 30, played and enjoyed a commendable debut, showing the sort of care in his use of the ball that established him as precisely the right sort of player for international football. Scotland, with their emphasis on avoiding error, are bound to make frequent use of such individuals.

In September 1997, however, his condition was a cause for concern. With the appointment of Wim Jansen as head coach, wholesale changes were being made at Celtic and McKinlay had not even appeared as a substitute since August 16.

Other trusted figures were also going through an awkward period. Gary McAllister's knee injury had prevented him playing for Coventry City since August 19, and his mere presence in the squad was a gratifying surprise, since it had been thought that he might have to drop out. John Collins, with a niggling thigh strain, had spent only limited time on the field at Monaco.

Some tinkering with the line-up looked sensible, but Brown preferred a bolder policy. All three men began the game, with the manager assuming that they could put Scotland in an unassailable position before any of them had to be replaced. McKinlay performed like a man in a hurry, bolting down the left wing and releasing an array of splendid crosses.

Belarus were beleaguered from the kick-off and conceded a goal in the sixth minute. In a variant of their familiar ploy, Collins touched a free-kick to McAllister, who shaped to hit a drive, but then turned away from an onrushing opponent before delivering his shot. Valeri Shantolosov blocked with his legs and Kevin Gallacher pounced to tuck away the rebound.

Although Petr Katchuro, of Sheffield United, slightly perturbed the defence, it was Scotland who devised an abundance of openings. Gordon Durie, whose injury forced his substitution at the interval, might have claimed a thrilling goal after hurling himself at another McKinlay cross, but the ball flew straight at the unprotected Shantolosov.

Super sub seals it

Eventually a change became unavoidable for Scotland and David Hopkin took over from the tiring McAllister. The midfielder, who had moved from Crystal Palace to Leeds United in the close season,

brought more with him from the substitutes' bench than a fresh supply of stamina.

He was involved in the move that saw Ally McCoist, a substitute, skew a shot across the face of the target and it was Hopkin, following up, who turned the ball into the net, via the inside of the post. Scotland, who had started to savour the victory, scored again soon afterwards, when Gallacher pursued Paul Lambert's chip and squeezed his finish home from a narrow angle.

There was a goal for Belarus, as Katchuro converted a penalty following Christian Dailly's push on Andrei Lavrik, but Scotland ended the match with a crescendo. With power and cunning, Hopkin took Craig Burley's pass to advance and wrong-foot Andrei Ostrovski with a swivel, before concluding the swaggering piece of play by drilling a shot into the corner of the net.

Hopkin's third cap had brought him his first two goals for his country. Despite the abundant satisfaction, the benefits of the result to Scotland were limited. Craig Brown's side were top of the group, but Austria, with a victory over Sweden the previous day, were only a point behind and had a game in hand.

The runners-up place in Group Four was now the feasible ambition for Scotland, but, for once in football, there was to be a great reward for coming second.

David Hopkin slots home his second goal after appearing as highly productive substitute against Belarus

SCOTLAND vs. LATVIA
Mission accomplished
October 11, 1997 (Celtic Park, Glasgow)

Painted faces can sometimes be a mask for fear. The audience at Celtic Park came kitted out for delight, but there was an undertow of apprehension. Gary McAllister felt the tug of that fear when he arrived in Glasgow to join the squad. The Scotland captain was surprised. Having come so far and surmounted many obstacles, he could not understand why anyone should expect failure in a home match against opponents whose form was vastly inferior. Perhaps it was the very promise of the scene that bred the disquiet.

Scotland were on the verge of fulfilment. Many of us may have struggled with basic arithmetic at school, but football makes better students of us all and the awkward calculations about the team's prospects had been made accurately. It was accepted that Austria, with only a home match against Belarus remaining, would win Group Four. They might not have been able to get the better of Craig Brown's team, but their results in other fixtures, including the two victories over Sweden, were outstanding.

As games were completed across the continent, though, it became ever more apparent that events were working in Scotland's favour. One place at the World Cup finals was available to the best of the runners-up in the nine European groups. Standings were established on the basis of results against the nations finishing first, third and fourth in each group. Amid much chewing of pencils and biting of finger nails, it was established that Scotland were virtually certain of automatic qualification for the 1998 finals so long as they beat Latvia.

Only an unthinkable defeat for Spain, in Gijon, at the hands of the Faroe Islands could prevent it. So it was that the crowd at Celtic Park were tantalized and, secretly, troubled. Having seen their side take such strides, failure against Latvia would have been unbearable.

It would have been convenient, given the stress in the stands, if Scotland could have brought relief with an early goal, but Craig Brown, at least, was in no hurry. He saw no advantage in bravado when all of the side's previous successes had been the product of methodical habits.

Latvia were shown the same respect as the other opponents. Scotland took them seriously and even detailed Paul Lambert to mark their playmaker, Vladimir Babicevs. There was nothing frivolous about the visitors either, even though the result would have no real consequence for Janis Gilis' team. Kevin Gallacher could gauge how earnest Latvia were, for he was often the subject of challenges from Jurijs Sevlakovs, a 38-year-old who showed that age need not deprive a centre-half of any of his severity.

In the seventh minute, McAllister broke through a tackle, swapped passes with Gallacher and spurted down the left to deliver a cross that Gordon Durie headed outside the post, but that incident was not a prelude to domination for Scotland. The first half was generally sedate, although there was a moment of queasiness for spectators when Jim Leighton had to turn behind a 30-yarder from Olegs Blagonadezdins. After half an hour, Scotland began to develop the momentum that carried them to a goal just before the interval.

Kevin Gallacher takes care in guiding the header that broke the deadlock against Latvia

Vital breakthrough

A Tom Boyd throw-in was guided on by Colin Hendry to John Collins. The midfielder's shot was too strong for Olegs Karavajevs to hold. The goalkeeper pushed the ball into the air, at a convenient height for Gallacher to head carefully into the net. It was the forward's sixth goal in five consecutive World Cup ties.

> **SCOTLAND 2**
> **LATVIA 0**
>
> **Scotland:**
> Leighton, Calderwood, Hendry, Dailly, Burley (W. McKinlay 89), G. McAllister, Lambert, Collins, Boyd (T. McKinlay 81), Durie (Donnelly 84), Gallacher.
>
> **Latvia:**
> Karvajevs, Lobanovs, Stepanovs, Sevlakovs, Bleidelis, Zemilinskis, Babicevs, Blagonadezdins (Stolcers 61), V. Ivanovs, Jelisejevs, (Rimkus 68), Pahars.
>
> **Scotland scorers:**
> Gallacher 43, Durie 80
>
> **Referee:**
> S. Piller (Hungary).

"After he scored," Brown was to say later, "there was no doubt in my mind that we would win. Our defensive record has been so good recently that I was convinced we would maintain our advantage."

Brown's side is not given to lapses and there may be special reasons for that unflagging vigilance. Of the 14 players used against Latvia, eight were aged 30 or over, yet they combine maturity with a youthful eagerness. Six of those established figures had never played in a match at the World Cup finals. Throughout the group fixtures they remembered that they were in the midst of their last chance.

McAllister was not spectacular against Latvia but his concentration did not wane. One of his tackles, on Andrejs Stolcers in the 66th minute, typified the alertness that allows Scotland to counter a threat before it has begun to develop.

There is, of course, uneasiness in the crowd when the side's need for that virtue is conspicuous and the fretfulness only ended when Gallacher displayed flair and technique to set up a second goal. Craig Burley's cross, ten minutes from the end, appeared to have caused no harm until the Blackburn Rovers striker guided a delicate chip over the goalkeeper. The ball bounced against the face of the crossbar and dropped to Durie, who headed home. With the last piece of irrational dread removed, jubilation was no longer to be kept at bay.

It would take a few more hours for clarification to arrive, in the shape of a 3–1 victory for Spain, but when the full-time whistle blew at Celtic Park, Scotland's feat in reaching the World Cup finals in France was already being acclaimed.

Saltires were draped round the shoulders of the players as they made their lap of honour at Celtic Park and Brown was inclined to let the scene speak for itself. His comments were restrained as he concentrated on thanking his backroom staff.

Identifying the key result in the campaign, the manager's mind did not turn to any of the tumultuous matches in Glasgow. "The game that we had to win," he said, "was the tough away one in Belarus. To go five weeks after the end of the Scottish season, take a team to Minsk and win 1–0 was outstanding."

Brown had created a side unsullied by boastfulness that had given the whole nation a cause for pride.

Gordon Durie enjoys his goal against Latvia. Scotland's task is completed

Facts and Figures

SCOTLAND'S 1998 WORLD CUP QUALIFYING CAMPAIGN

Date	Opponent	Venue	Result	Score	Scorers	Att.
31.8.96	Austria	A	D	0–0		29,500
5.10.96	Latvia	A	W	2–0	Collins, Jackson	9,500
9.10.96	Estonia	A	Abandoned			
10.11.96	Sweden	H	W	1–0	McGinlay	46,738
11.2.97	Estonia	N*	D	0–0		4,000
29.3.97	Estonia	H	W	2–0	Boyd, Meet (o.g.)	17,996
2.4.97	Austria	H	W	2–0	Gallacher (2)	43,295
30.4.97	Sweden	A	L	1–2	Gallacher	40,000
8.6.97	Belarus	A	W	1–0	G. McAllister (pen.)	12,000
7.9.97	Belarus	H	W	4–1	Gallacher (2), Hopkin (2)	20,135
11.10.97	Latvia	H	W	2–0	Gallacher, Durie	47,613

N* = match played at neutral venue, Monaco

APPEARANCES AND GOALSCORERS

Players	Apps (Max 10)	Sub	Goals (15)
Tom Boyd	10		1
Craig Burley	9		
Colin Calderwood	9		
John Collins	8		1
Christian Dailly	3		
Billy Dodds		3	
Simon Donnelly		1	
Gordon Durie	3	2	1
Duncan Ferguson	2		
Ian Ferguson		1	
Kevin Gallacher	7	1	6
Scot Gemmill	1	2	
Andy Goram	3		
Colin Hendry	7		
David Hopkin	1	1	2
Darren Jackson	6		1
Paul Lambert	5	2	
Jim Leighton	7		
Brian McAllister		1	
Gary McAllister	9		1
Stuart McCall	2		
Ally McCoist	1	4	
John McGinlay	2	2	1
Tosh McKinlay	8	2	
Billy McKinlay	1	2	
Jackie McNamara	2	1	
Paul McStay	2		
John Spencer	1		
Derek Whyte	1		
Own goals			1

GROUP 4 FINAL TABLE

Teams	P	W	D	L	F	A	Pts
Austria	10	8	1	1	17	4	25
Scotland	10	7	2	1	15	3	23
Sweden	10	7	0	3	16	9	21
Latvia	10	3	1	6	10	14	10
Estonia	10	1	1	8	4	16	4
Belarus	10	1	1	8	5	21	4

**Only the durable Tom Boyd
started all ten qualifiers**

Chapter 3
World Cup Stars

The players who took their ecstatic, tired steps from the field at Celtic Park in October must have thought that they had qualified for the World Cup finals. A few months on, they have had time to think again. Scotland will certainly be in action this summer, but there are no guarantees that any particular player will be in the squad. They have won their qualifying games, but now they have to keep on winning the approval of the manager.

Craig Brown is not fickle and there is a core group that he would prefer to keep together. This, after all, is hardly the moment for dabbling. Last November, he picked a party of 26 for a friendly with France in Saint-Etienne.

When you consider that four of them would have to be removed before a squad of 22 could be named for the World Cup finals, then it might seem impossible for any outsiders to break their way into Brown's schemes.

Football, however, disrupts everyone's intentions. The manager has no wish to tamper with a defence that has been so effective, but he must weigh up

events at each person's club. Had Christian Gross, for example, concluded, after taking over at Tottenham Hotspur, that he should ditch Colin Calderwood, then Brown would have been uneasy about the readiness of a player who ought to be one of the mainstays in France. An international manager appears to wield great power, but is really at the mercy of decisions made elsewhere.

Nucleus in every position

Ideally, Brown would like to keep his nucleus of players and then add younger men whose time to serve Scotland will really come in the years ahead. The pattern is already discernible. He has established contenders for the goalkeeper's position, but Wimbledon's Neil Sullivan has emerged to join them.

Christian Dailly, the Derby County centre-back, has taken greater steps still and should play in France. Only injuries, such as the broken jaw that Dailly suffered, could really harm some of Brown's plans. If he were the sort of person who was prone to anxiety, he would focus his concern on the forwards. Rangers' record goalscorer Ally McCoist, at 35, is bedevilled by injuries, while Gordon Durie and Darren Jackson will need to get enough minutes under their belts at, respectively, Rangers and Celtic, where each tends to be a substitute. Of the strikers, only Kevin Gallacher of Blackburn gives no cause for worry. Brown needs to find other candidates and will have to weigh up the claims of men such as Scott Booth at Utrecht. The preparations for France 1998 may be as taxing as the tournament itself.

With rebuilding in progress, the squad could only return to Hampden for training during the qualifiers

Tom **Boyd**

When Tom Boyd, who was captain for the evening, led out the team for their friendly with France at the end of last year, he was playing his 24th consecutive match for Scotland. Such an unbroken run is an act of defiance against everything we have come to expect of modern football.

Familiar face: Tom Boyd reached his 50th cap after a mere seven years with Scotland

It is supposed to be inevitable that the grinding abundance of games in club competitions will exhaust players or, at the very least, injure them. If all else fails, those yellow cards that flash like strobe lights through most matches will normally force a man out of action. Again, Boyd is the exception. He does not seem to pick up suspensions easily for Scotland.

The defender was the only person to be in the starting line-up for all 10 of the qualifying games for the 1998 World Cup. Boyd is hardly allowed a moment for recuperation, as you can see by checking his whereabouts over recent summers.

In June 1997, he was part of the dogged, rearguard action that eked out the 1–0 victory for Scotland in Minsk. The year before, he was fully occupied in the effort to deal with Holland, England and Switzerland at Euro 96. At 32, his hardiness is undiminished. Craig Brown is obliged to put up with a whirl of withdrawals and assorted disruptions, but Boyd remains the still point around which all the changes to the team revolve. Yet if he now looks indispensable, there was a time when Scotland failed to find a use for him.

Tom BOYD	
Born:	November 24, 1965
Birthplace:	Glasgow
Height:	5ft 11in.
Weight:	11st. 4lb
Age:	32
Position:	Defender
Club record:	Motherwell, Chelsea, Celtic
International record:	51 caps, 1 goal
Scotland debut:	vs. Romania, September 12, 1990 (2–1 victory)

Late starter

In common with several others in the squad, Boyd was a late-starter at international level. As a Motherwell player he made five appearances for the under-21 team, but there were few signs that further promotion was likely.

When Andy Roxburgh, the then Scotland manager, chose him for a B international against Yugoslavia in 1990, there were some who took the jaundiced view that he was only being picked because the match was at Fir Park, his home ground, and there was a need to tempt the locals into attending. The cynicism was dispelled that evening by a performance of such energy from Boyd that it sparked excitement in every spectator.

The momentum was not quite sufficient to pitch him into the squad for the 1990 World Cup finals, but he did make his first appearance, against Romania as a substitute, in September of that year. Scotland's squad was particularly impaired by withdrawals, but it proved to be one of those occasions when adversity only makes a side more stubborn. Boyd set up the winner for Ally McCoist in a 2–1 victory.

Nowadays, Boyd is so familiar a figure with Scotland that he is scarcely noticed at all. A down-to-earth view of his duties also tends to discourage attention. Against Estonia in March of 1997, he scored his first international goal and also hit the bar, prompting a journalist to ask playfully whether he now fancied himself as a forward. "Steady," responded Boyd, urging a return to realism.

He has cause to be happy enough with his own line of work. During the mid-1990s, for example, when Andrei Kanchelskis was at his most celebrated with Manchester United, Boyd closed the Russian winger out of the game in each of the three internationals that pitted them against one another.

In his unobtrusive way, Boyd has enjoyed several outstanding experiences in football. Having joined Motherwell as a youth trainee, he went on, as a 25-year-old, to captain the club to its triumph in the 1991 Tennents Scottish Cup Final.

It was his last appearance for the Fir Park team before signing for Chelsea in an £800,000 transfer. Boyd soon returned to Scotland, joining Celtic in the swap deal that took Tony Cascarino to Stamford Bridge. With the Glasgow club there has been more of the low-profile success in which he specializes. The defender became Celtic's captain last summer, following Paul McStay's retirement, and by November had collected his first trophy, the Coca-Cola Cup.

Opinions may fluctuate among supporters, but Boyd is always in fashion with managers. Although naturally right-footed, he developed in senior football as a left-back and recently, has slipped infield to central defence, the position he occupied in his boyhood. Given the variety of ways in which he can give sound service, it is natural that coaches are quick to jot down Boyd's name as they make their plans.

He also embodies a tradition. Walter Smith, the Rangers manager, has dealt heavily in overseas signings, but he admitted that Scottish football would be poorer if it lost the dedicated local lads who give a club its identity. When Smith tried to think of the epitome of such characters, Tom Boyd's name was the first on his lips.

Despite filling a variety of roles, Boyd's efficiency for Scotland has rarely wavered

Craig **Burley**

Craig Burley had to go to Japan to catch the eye of his fellow countrymen. That circuitous route was his path to the international side as he made his debut for Scotland at the Kirin Cup in May 1995.

It was a taxing journey that indicated the length Craig Brown must go to when he is scrambling for fresh players. For the manager, the main prize at that little tournament lay in his discovery of people who might be used in the patched-up team for a European Championship qualifier against the Faroe Islands the following month.

In that goalless draw with Japan, Burley and Paul Lambert were among those earning their first caps. Their emergence in that remote venue was further proof of this country's knack of uncovering surprising new candidates for the Scotland side. Lambert, at least, was well-known with Motherwell as a regular member of the cast in domestic football, but Burley had always been employed south of the border, and supporters might have struggled to put a face to the name.

He had gone straight from school to join Chelsea. Over the decades, a huge number of youngsters have taken this sort of step and it has been pointed out that the Scots used to be the foreigners of English football. Now, in the cosmopolitan Premiership, the imports come from much further away and Burley was something of a rarity in his years at Stamford Bridge.

Craig BURLEY	
Born: September 24, 1971	
Birthplace: Ayr	
Height: 5ft 11½ in.	
Weight: 12st. 13lb	
Age: 26	
Position: Midfielder	
Club record:	
Chelsea, Celtic	
International record:	
23 caps, 0 goals	
Scotland debut:	
vs. Japan, May 21, 1995	
(0–0 draw)	

Bucking the trend

Few Scots come all the way through the youth system at an English club and proceed to the highest level. Back in his homeland, the public may only have been vaguely aware of the fact, but Burley fully established himself at Chelsea.

Even after the influx of foreign stars under Ruud Gullit's regime, he still appeared in 31 of the club's League fixtures in the 1996–97 season. The Dutch manager was famous, however, for his readiness to keep team selection in a constant state of flux and there was no place for Burley in the side that beat Middlesbrough to win the 1997 FA Cup. It was Chelsea's first trophy in 26 years and one might have expected to find Burley desolate after his exclusion from the achievement, but he is even-tempered about the affair and claims it amounted to nothing more than a few bad hours.

After the Final, he was asked if he would still be joining the club's end of season tour to the Far East. Burley was content to do so and remembers putting the whole episode behind him while having a few drinks with his celebrating team-mates on the flight.

Craig Burley is rapidly turning into one of the senior members of the squad

Burley has the physique and resolve for one of the most taxing jobs in the side

The Scot was far from indifferent to his omission from the Cup Final, but he has too much pride to allow himself to wallow in misery. There is a self-confidence about Burley that adds to a team's spirit.

When he moved to Celtic last year, the presumption was that Burley would be used to anchor the midfield, but that deduction underestimated the adventurous instincts that were waiting to find expression. By the beginning of 1998 he had scored 10 goals for Celtic, including a double against FC Tirol in a tumultuous 6–3 UEFA Cup victory, the winner in the Coca-Cola Cup semi-final, the header that killed off Dundee United in the Final itself, the only goal of the match with then-leaders Hearts in December and the opener in the Old Firm game on January 2.

Considering that last effort, Charlie Nicholas, the former Scotland player, noted that Burley has a forward's instinct in the penalty area that prevents him from rushing a shot. There have been suggestions that his country should also use him in an advanced mid-field position, but it was not a new idea to Craig Brown, who had already fielded Burley in the centre of the pitch for the match with Sweden at Ibrox. At half-time, however, he was switched to the wing-back role he normally occupies for his country.

Although Burley is also valuable at centre-back, as he showed in the 1–0 win over Belarus in Minsk, the 26-year-old probably serves Scotland's present needs best when he is playing on the flanks. Brown is a devotee of the 3–5–2 formation that, in theory, asks a single player on each wing to patrol the entire length of the pitch. Burley has the stamina to cope and the flexibility to remain effective whether he is tackling an opponent or embarking on a forward run of his own. The consistency of Scotland's results owes a great deal to reliable performers such as Burley.

Because of the long involvement with Chelsea, the Scotland fans initially had only a superficial understanding of his merits, but they are increasingly happy to get better acquainted with Burley.

Colin **Calderwood**

It is an honour to be chosen to represent your country, but a man does not always get the chance to savour the occasion for long. The anthems had barely ceased playing before Colin Calderwood discovered the tribulations of international football on a chilly night in Moscow. Russia were intent on wrenching the Scotland team out of shape.

"They kept pulling me out to the right-back position where I was facing some guy who was lightning quick," he said, "and all I wanted was to be in the middle with a forward tight against me. I was shouting over to the bench, but they just ignored me."

Although he may have felt abandoned, the Tottenham Hotspur centre-half was really being trusted. No matter how much advice is given beforehand it is the player himself who must acclimatize himself to the highest levels of the game. Scotland appreciated how sure-footed Calderwood had been in completing his long climb through all the ranks of his profession. He was already 30 by the time he made that debut against Russia. His place of birth made it difficult to attract the sort of interest from scouts that would have allowed the beginning of an ascent at a major club.

He grew up in the south-west corner of the country and did not even get the chance to sign for his local heroes. Calderwood is still a passionate supporter of Stranraer and makes a nuisance of himself on the Spurs team bus by insisting that the radio be kept on until the announcer has completed the Scottish Second Division scores. While growing up, the present he always sought was a season ticket for Stair Park. A spot on the terracing was easier for him to attain than a place in the team because his home-town club did not run a youth development scheme.

After playing with Ayr United boys club, he moved first to Mansfield Town and then to Swindon Town, who were still in the old Fourth Division at the time.

Calderwood captained the club through its ascent until, under Glenn Hoddle's management, promotion to the Premiership was clinched in 1993. The defender went on to sign for Spurs and his development had come to the notice of Craig Brown while he was still Andy Roxburgh's assistant. In that period, Calderwood represented no more than an interesting possibility for the Scotland team.

Even so, Brown was intrigued by the thought of employing Calderwood at international level. No matter what other deficiencies there may be, Scotland never has any difficulty in providing openings for prospective internationals. The numerous call-offs ensure plenty of vacancies.

Colin CALDERWOOD

Born: January 20, 1965
Birthplace: Stranraer
Height: 6ft
Weight: 13st.
Age: 33
Position: Centre-back
Club record:
  Mansfield Town, Swindon Town, Tottenham Hotspur
International record:
  24 caps, 1 goal
Scotland debut:
  vs. Russia, March 29, 1995 (0–0 draw)

Colin Calderwood's late development makes him fight all the harder to hold on to success

Opponents are brushed aside when Calderwood sets his mind on winning the ball

Making a point

Calderwood filled one of them in that European Championship tie with Russia and, despite his self-deprecating account of the game, Scotland kept a clean sheet and took back a point from Moscow. Brown's hunch that the centre-half would prove sound had been vindicated.

Calderwood is the type of player who long ago removed all pretensions from his game. His touch is good enough for Spurs, since the appointment of Christian Gross as manager, to employ him as a midfield player, but his purposefulness is most evident when one sees the stark determination with which he marks an opponent. He is tough in the genuine, respectable sense. When he makes a challenge every ounce of his energies goes into that bid to be first to the ball. No apologies, no concessions, no compromises.

He is one of the people in Brown's squad whose place in their club side has been in doubt, putting in jeopardy their hopes of taking part in the World Cup finals. The resolve with which Calderwood attends to business, however, can only assist him in the bid to be in the party for France.

Given how formidable he can be on the field, his placidity in every other respect comes as a surprise. Brown himself was certainly taken aback by it on the trip to America prior to Euro 96, when the manager and defender found themselves competing against one another on the golf course.

Brown's chip had finished six feet from the flag and he was staring glumly at the outcome when Calderwood conceded the putt. The chivalrous behaviour seems less bewildering when you see the mild-mannered way in which the centre-half wanders around hotels while on foreign trips with Scotland. Aggression is not to be squandered when it can be put to such valuable service on the pitch. Calderwood transforms himself as he prepares for a game.

Hoddle encouraged players to take a quiet moment to think about the task ahead, but the defender goes even further and sometimes slaps himself in the face to heighten concentration. Forwards who know him as a daunting adversary might find Calderwood even more intimidating if they ever saw him in the dressing room.

John **Collins**

A caller to John Collins' apartment in Monaco in the autumn of 1996 found his daughter answering the phone with a confident "Bonjour."

Although Julia was only three years old at the time, it came as no surprise to find that the midfielder's family were eager learners. They are taking after their father. When Collins moved from Celtic to AS Monaco in the close season of 1996 everyone knew that he would adapt well, even though British players are notorious for their difficulties in fitting in at clubs on the continent.

John COLLINS

Born: January 31, 1968
Birthplace: Galashiels
Height: 5ft 7in.
Weight: 10st. 10lb
Age: 30
Position: Midfielder
Club record:
    Hibernian, Celtic,
    AS Monaco
International record:
    46 caps, 9 goals
Scotland debut:
    vs. Saudi Arabia, February
    17, 1988 (2–2 draw)

Poor Ian Rush still gets ridiculed for his observation, after his transfer to Juventus, that being in Italy was "like living in a foreign country." By contrast, Collins relishes the culture he has entered. Within a few weeks of his arrival in Monaco he was giving interviews in French to the local television stations. The men who have taken advantage of the Bosman ruling appreciate the wealth it can bring, but Collins is to be believed when he asserts that he always wanted the chance to play abroad in any case.

Although Monaco arranged for a language tutor to live with him and his family for a while, the player was a successful student because of his own yearning to speak French. The urge for self-improvement has always been strong. His natural aptitude for the game has been enhanced by a desire to make the most of himself. At 5ft 7in., he is small for a successful athlete, but he has developed a physique with the lithe power of a boxer.

While adding muscle to his body, Collins was also extending the range of the contribution he could make on the field. The neatness of touch attracted Celtic, who bought him from Hibernian for almost £1 million in 1990, but he reacted impressively when Liam Brady, who was appointed manager a year later, insisted that he should be able to score a greater number of goals. His penchant for finding the net gradually became an important weapon for the club.

John Collins concludes a clever ploy to score the opener in Latvia

Goalscorer and goal-maker

It has been wielded to similar effect for his country. Collins is a clean striker of the ball and is often involved in the free-kicks around the area. One manoeuvre on the edge of the box ended with him putting Scotland ahead against Latvia in Riga during the qualifiers for the 1998 World Cup. He was to punish the same opposition at Celtic Park when he delivered a long-range drive that forced the parry from which Kevin Gallacher scored. His appreciation of the game makes him dangerous in a variety of ways.

Collins removed the possibility of frustration in an away match with San Marino, during the qualifiers for Euro 96, when he was quick-witted enough to see that defenders were backing away in the expectation that he would release the ball. Instead, Collins darted straight through them to complete his run by giving Scotland the lead. Although his absence is unimaginable at present, Collins's involvement with the national team was once subject to interruption.

He missed the finals of the 1992 European Championship when it was felt that he would not be happy in the role on the left flank that was then on offer to him. Scotland's tactical system has subsequently changed and Collins occupies a slightly more central position, with a wing-back operating outside him. In every sense, the midfielder has found his place in the scheme of things. In his first year at Monaco, Collins won a French League championship medal and was part of the side that defeated Newcastle United on its way to the UEFA Cup semi-finals.

Monaco won their group in the 1997–98 Champions League to progress to the latter stages of the European Cup. His experiences with Jean Tigana's side have satisfied not only Collins's aspirations, but also his curiosity. In his days with Celtic, he had been puzzled by the explosiveness of continental teams.

"At times we felt we were containing them and then – bang! – they would break right through you," he said of one match against Paris Saint-Germain.

With Monaco he has explored the mystery, going through the exercises designed to give spring to the calves and hamstrings, experiencing the computer tests that identify which muscles need to be strengthened, and providing the blood samples that are examined to determine which minerals and vitamins he might need. Collins is engrossed by it all and regrets only the fact that the strict regime in the team hotel forbids him to eat ice cream.

He jokes that he plans to return to Scottish football so that he can have as much ice cream as he wants and play as a 15-stone midfielder. In the healthy sense, though, Collins already is a player of real substance.

Collins's timing of a shot has brought goals and provided six-yard box ricochets for the forwards

Gordon **Durie**

After he had netted a header against Latvia, ensuring Scotland's place at the World Cup finals, Gordon Durie raced away in delight. He was a little unfortunate in his choice of direction. He found himself sprinting towards the dug-out, where Ally McCoist, a substitute, waited to greet him.

"Well done, Gordon," said his mischievous Rangers team-mate, "that's two goals in two years." McCoist was guilty of exaggeration, but Durie has needed great patience to build a substantial international career.

Few players can sustain an involvement with their country over a period of 11 years. Durie made his debut for Scotland in 1987, as a substitute in a 1–0 win over Bulgaria. Such longevity is always noteworthy, but it becomes remarkable when one considers the disruptions he has had to endure. When a powerful running style is applied in a contact sport, injuries are

Gordon DURIE
Born: December 6, 1965
Birthplace: Paisley
Height: 5ft 10in.
Weight: 12st. 13lb
Age: 32
Position: Forward
Club record:
East Fife, Hibernian, Chelsea, Tottenham Hotspur, Rangers
International record:
38 caps, 7 goals
Scotland debut:
vs. Bulgaria, November 11, 1987 (1–0 victory)

inevitable and Durie has coped with long lay-offs and an occasional need for surgery.

Since signing for Rangers in 1993, the forward has also had to battle for a place in the team at Ibrox. At so successful and wealthy a club, with its large squad, few players can ever feel sure of selection, but it is difficult for anyone to catch the eye of a national manager if they are not being picked regularly. Although Durie won his 38th cap against France in November of last year, those appearances for Scotland have been amassed through perseverance.

For various reasons, Durie spent two years out of

Gordon Durie is a strong runner in attack and has shown stamina too to revive his international career

Durie's dynamic first-half display against Belarus paved the way for a 4–1 victory at Pittodrie

the national team before returning to his country's colours in the spring of 1996. His form at club level forced him back into international consideration, especially when he became only the third man to claim a hat-trick in a Scottish Cup Final.

His comeback began in a lowly B international in Denmark in April, but his impact was sufficient to ensure, two months later, that he started all three of Scotland's matches at the European Championship in England. Durie has shown resilience to keep on pressing his claim but he is assisted by the durable impression that he has made on managers.

Durie's first club was East Fife and Dave Clarke, the man who persuaded him to come to Bayview in 1981, experienced intense delight on leaving the Durie household with the youngster's signature. Clarke remembers that he virtually skipped along the street in sheer satisfaction over his coup because he knew he

had secured the sort of talent that is usually earmarked for one or other member of the Old Firm. Subsequent managers may have been more circumspect in their reactions, but they, too, have a strong regard for the player.

Man in demand

He has always been in demand, moving from East Fife to Hibernian to Chelsea to Tottenham Hotspur. Terry Venables, who took Durie to White Hart Lane in 1991, thinks that the striker will make an impact at the 1998 World Cup and admitted that only Durie's desire to return to his homeland saw him leave Spurs at all.

The men who have managed him at international level are just as eloquent in their approval. Scotland forwards can expect to be disparaged for their scoring records, even though they frequently face daunting adversaries and are supplied with a limited number of chances. Durie's worth has been fully recognized by Craig Brown, who sent the forward to represent Scotland in the Europe vs. The Rest of the World match that preceded the draw for the World Cup finals in Marseille.

He is not a natural penalty area predator, but the scope for poaching is limited, in any case, by the use that has been made of him. Scotland have lacked wingers of true international quality for many years and sometimes it was Durie, with his pace and stamina, who was asked to play wide in midfield. On occasion, though, a formidable prowess in the role of principal striker could be glimpsed.

Without Durie, Scotland would probably not have made it to the 1992 European Championship. The team was 2–0 down to Switzerland at half-time a qualifier in Berne. Durie was then switched from the wing to the centre-forward position and induced immediate panic in the opposition. He scored after just two minutes of the second half and created the opportunity for McCoist to equalize with seven minutes remaining. Scotland drew 2–2 that night and eventually finished a single point ahead of Switzerland in the group.

At Ibrox, he gets teased over his failings as a card player. Observing a queue on a street in Romania during one trip, McCoist cried, "They're all waiting for a game of cards with 'Juke Box'."

In football, however, it is those who have gambled against the durable Durie who have been the losers.

Kevin **Gallacher**

Kevin Gallacher intends to be 26 forever.

The forward does not propose to lie about his age, but he believes he is entitled to quarrel with his birth certificate. The broken leg he suffered in 1994 was fractured again when he attempted a comeback and Gallacher hardly played for two seasons.

"I don't know where ages 27 and 28 went," he said. Because of the interruption, he still thinks of himself as the 26-year-old he was before the injuries. Anyone who has watched him recently will go along with that line of thinking.

The sticklers for detail, and the calendar, will insist that he is 31, but Gallacher does not resemble a veteran at all. If the striker has changed, it is only by improving.

In February, 1997, he was a player with 26 caps and a paltry two goals for Scotland to his credit. But in the half-dozen World Cup qualifiers which followed, Gallacher scored six times. The goals were timely, just as Maurice Johnston's had been in the qualifiers for Italia 90. It was Gallacher's sequence that piloted Scotland to the finals in France.

Kevin Gallacher (left) can celebrate qualification and his own rise to prominence

His pair of goals was the tempest that sunk Austria at Celtic Park. It was Gallacher, too, who broke the deadlock in the home matches with Belarus and Latvia. The exploits also illustrated the mature range of skills that was forged, in part, by his unhappy experiences.

Gaining from adversity

"What those injuries gave me," the forward explained, "was a left foot. When I was recovering, I wasn't allowed to kick the ball with my right foot and I spent so much time using the left that it became my better one for a while." It has not grown dull from disuse since, as Gallacher showed with the exquisite chip against the crossbar that led to Gordon Durie scoring against Latvia.

Developments at Ewood Park have also nudged him into greater prominence. Magnificent though Alan Shearer can be as a one-man forward line, he sometimes seemed to suck up all the oxygen in the penalty area, leaving the other Blackburn strikers to faint away. Gallacher is full of praise for the Englishman, but knows that he, Mike Newell and Chris Sutton found themselves orbiting around Shearer.

In the wake of the centre-forward's transfer to Newcastle United in 1996, Blackburn have reverted to more conventional pairings in attack and Gallacher has claimed his share of goals, particularly since Roy Hodgson took over as manager last year.

Many people in Scotland previously failed to appreciate that putting the ball in the net was part of his trade. In some quarters, he still gets spoken of as a winger.

"It must be because I'm small and quick," Gallacher said with a degree of bewilderment. "When I was just starting out with Dundee United, Jim McLean used to put me on the wing, but that was really just part of my education." Of course, he did score the winner for United

Kevin GALLACHER
Born: November 23, 1966
Birthplace: Clydebank
Height: 5ft 8in.
Weight: 11st. 3lb
Age: 31
Position: Forward
Club record:
Dundee United, Coventry City, Blackburn Rovers
International record:
34 caps, 8 goals
Scotland debut:
vs. Colombia, May 17, 1988 (0–0 draw)

Gallacher should be used to scoring but the thrill of putting Scotland ahead against Latvia was still great

against Barcelona in 1987 with an effort delivered from the right touchline. It was definitely a shot, not a misplaced cross. Ask any Tannadice fan.

At Coventry City and Blackburn, whom he joined in a £1.5 million transfer, he has considered himself a central forward. Craig Brown has often asked him to play in a wide position, but Gallacher was content to do so only because he was serving the team's needs.

The fact that he was frequently marooned on the flank or used only as a substitute has led to some misapprehensions about his record. "If you counted up the minutes I'd spent in the middle of the attack it wouldn't amount to much," said Gallacher. "I tried to explain that, but nobody really cared."

Things have changed. Whether accompanied by Darren Jackson or Gordon Durie, he is a member, nowadays, of a centre-forward partnership that is full of energy and mobility.

"It shows you don't necessarily need a big target man," he said, "though it's good to have that option. Scotland are playing a more European build-up and it suits me." There is an exhilaration about Gallacher that has borne fruit in the variety of goals he has scored, going from a thunderous half-volley against Austria, to the six-yard box pilfering in the matches with Belarus and Latvia.

It is the instinct for the latter sort of opportunity that makes a striker persistently dangerous, and Gallacher suspects he is custom-built for such situations. "Being small and quick," he admits, "I sometimes get through gaps and reach the loose ball first."

Gallacher has been playing international football for 10 years, but he is presently in the best form of his life. Scotland will be delighted to believe that he truly has turned back the hands of his body clock.

Andy Goram

Early in 1996, shortly after Andy Goram had produced his habitual virtuosity against Celtic, Walter Smith, the Rangers manager, was engaged in a conversation that began as a playful attempt to remember the last mistake the goalkeeper had made.

The discussion grew ever more serious as the difficulty of finding an unadulterated error became apparent. An effort of archaeological excavation was needed to reach some distant recollections of the difficulties Goram experienced just after he joined the club, from Hibernian, in 1991.

You could argue, in 1996, that he had been flawless for five years. Along with Jim Leighton, he has helped demolish the stereotype that claims a Scottish goalkeeper cannot go for more than a game or two without committing a howler. The image always was a travesty and it is easy to pick out men such as Bill Brown, in the 1960s, and David Harvey, in the 1970s, who have served the national team very well. With the increasing prominence of Scotland in the current decade, however, Leighton and Goram have had a better chance of achieving widespread respect.

The Rangers goalkeeper was one of the men singled out when Howard Wilkinson recited a rueful litany after his Leeds United team had been knocked out of the European Cup by the Ibrox club in 1992.

"It was like trying to carry a ton weight up the down escalator," he said. "Goram, outstanding… you wonder how Scotland could ever lose a football match." Not even Goram can always make Craig Brown's side impervious to defeat, but there have been many occasions on which he has looked just as invincible as Wilkinson suspected.

Goram has all the attributes you might expect. The quickfire reactions produce a stream of spectacular saves because he begins to move a split second faster than an ordinary goalkeeper can. His hand-eye co-ordination is highly refined and he was a proficient cricketer until Rangers' fear of the broken fingers he might sustain while pursuing that summertime recreation became too great for him to be allowed to continue. He also possesses the sort of nimble feet that would allow him to dance down the wicket.

Andy GORAM	
Born:	April 13, 1964
Birthplace:	Bury
Height:	5ft 11in.
Weight:	12st. 13lb
Age:	33
Position:	Goalkeeper
Club record:	Oldham Athletic, Hibernian, Rangers
International record:	42 caps, 0 goals
Scotland debut:	vs. East Germany, October 16, 1985 (0–0 draw)

Andy Goram has been a principal contributor in building Scotland's superb defensive record

Technical perfection

They are put to good use before football's larger audiences as he is quick to get himself into the perfect position. The expert eye also recognizes skills of which the rest of us, with our lack of specialist knowledge, are probably unaware. Leighton says that he cannot think of another goalkeeper who is so technically correct in every facet of the profession. Forwards, even if they cannot analyse the science, are acutely aware of its consequences.

When a striker is clean through, he will often lift his shot a little so that it rises above the goalkeeper's dive, but even as he is falling to the ground Goram has a knack of somehow thrusting up an arm and blocking the ball. After yet another display of those arts, Tommy Burns, who was then in charge of Celtic, announced that it would say on his tombstone that Goram had broken his heart. In all candour, however, it must be conceded that the goalkeeper has sometimes pained his own manager as well.

Smith, citing problems with the player's attitude to recovering fitness after an injury, actually put him on the transfer list in 1994, although the whole exercise could have been intended as a shock tactic. If so, it must have been a success, given that he remains a Rangers player four years later. Goram might also regret a few of the headlines in which he has appeared, but he is not the kind of person who will be undermined by anxiety.

The goalkeeper has a detestation of seeing the ball go past him, but that intensity is coupled with a relaxed air when he is not actually in action. There is one photo that shows him taking a nonchalant swig of a sports drink. It is the sort of posture a man might adopt after a raid on the fridge in his kitchen, but Goram was in the midst of an Old Firm game at the time. Not even he can always be quite so equable as that ,and the goalkeeper has had to deal with operations and fears over his future in the past few years.

In 1995, Scotland acceded to his request to be released from the squad for a match with Belarus after Goram had said he was not mentally attuned to take part. His service to the team has continued all the same and he made marvellous saves that underpinned Scotland's win over Latvia in Riga during the World Cup qualifier.

In the months ahead, the contest with Leighton for the goalkeeper's position will be hard-fought even if it is also filled with mutual admiration.

A steely concentration makes Goram capable of the extraordinary save even after long spells of inactivity

Colin **Hendry**

As a crucial moment in the World Cup qualifying campaign approached, one newspaper tried to rally the nation by printing a Colin Hendry mask. It was supposed to be cut out and glued to the back of a cereal packet before being worn.

Although few people went to quite such lengths, the choice of image had been perfect. The centre-half is the face of Scotland, just as Joe Jordan was in the 1970s. Unlike the forward of yesteryear, Hendry has not had to lose some prominent teeth to become an icon.

Genetics and fortunate timing were on his side. Fair hair and a mighty physique are a boon to a sportsman in the "Braveheart" era. As a highly agreeable person, Hendry is even willing to strike some Mel Gibson poses for the camera. Despite that, he will never be accused of posturing.

There is no pretence about him on the field and the battles he fights there do not benefit from special effects. The effort and the blows are all authentic. Hendry cannot help but be vivid.

He argues that he has never had any chance of hiding his place on the pitch. The defender wryly points out that if he makes a mistake everyone in the ground knows exactly who the guilty party was.

Hendry may be right, but it is not only because of his blond head that he stands out. From the man-trap snap of his tackles to the sinew-stretching lunge of his interceptions, there is drama to his performance. The only wonder is that it took so long for him to stand in the spotlight.

Hendry was 27 before he began playing for the full Scotland team in 1993. Despite that late start there had

Colin Hendry has bought a channelled passion to Scotland's cause

been no oversight by the SFA coaching staff, who had opened files on him long before that debut. He had been in the Scotland side for a B match against East Germany in 1990. On that occasion, Hendry caught the eye, as he always does, but left the onlooker bemused. The main impression of the player, then with Manchester City, was of thunderous energy.

Duel ambition

It was stirring to see him go romping down the wing in his eagerness to affect the game, but you knew that this sort of ungoverned enthusiasm would not appeal to anyone charged with running the national team. Hendry, in the early days of his career, had acquired an ambition to be involved in every duel in every area of the pitch. At his first club, Dundee, it was not clear whether he would settle down as a centre-half or a centre-forward.

He has always had an overwhelming zeal. So eager was he to sign for Blackburn Rovers, once Dundee had accepted an offer of £25,000, that Hendry only thought to ask where Blackburn was after he had completed the deal. They told him that it was near Preston, but he admits that he was none the wiser for that information. If you wish to understand Hendry you need to know about the background to his boyhood in the Highland town of Keith.

He saw his father start a shift as a postman at 6.00 a.m. before working as a driving school instructor in the afternoon. Time was also spent helping out in the shop that Hendry's mother ran. Any spare hours in his father's schedule were filled with voluntary labour for the boys' team or with his activities as a councillor. It isn't hard to guess how his son got the impression that it might be possible to fill every position on the pitch. Exhilarating though such adventurousness can be, Hendry was really dissipating his energy.

In his second spell with Blackburn, he came under

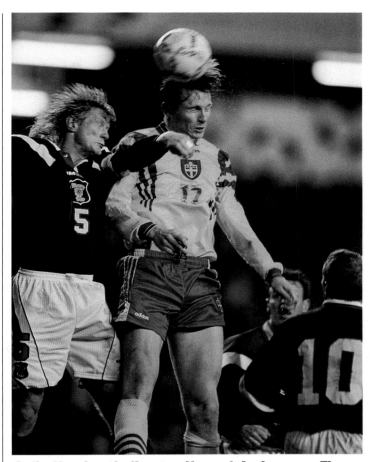

Colin Hendry challenges Kennet Andersson. The defender is trusted to rise to every occasion

Colin HENDRY	
Born: December 7, 1965	
Birthplace: Keith	
Height: 6ft 1in.	
Weight: 12st. 7lb	
Age: 32	
Position: Centre-back	
Club record:	
Dundee, Blackburn Rovers,	
Manchester City,	
Blackburn Rovers	
International record:	
28 caps, 1 goal	
Scotland debut:	
vs. Estonia, May 19, 1993	
(3–0 victory)	

the influence of Kenny Dalglish and his coach Ray Harford. They wanted him to focus solely on his duties as a centre-back and let others attend to whatever else is required in a game. Hendry had reached the age when wisdom makes it easier to accept good advice. The records may seem to chronicle his gradual decline as a goalscorer, but they are really registering his progress as a defender.

Blackburn won the title, suffered a dip in performance thereafter and are now gathering strength again, yet throughout the fluctuations Hendry has been admirable, receiving accolades not only for his power but also for his clean tackling. Such footballers are coveted and he used to wonder about the rumours that linked him with many clubs, including Rangers. A conversation with Jack Walker, Blackburn's millionaire owner, left him in no doubt, however, that any attempt to buy him would be repelled.

Hendry was content to hear that. For the national team's part, Scotland should simply be happy that they are entitled to borrow him from Blackburn now and again.

Paul **Lambert**

Paul Lambert had a long wait before his gifts were fully recognized, but nowadays it is the clubs that seek his services who must bide their time.

There were weeks of speculation prior to Lambert's £1.75 million transfer to Celtic in November, but behind the scenes the deal had already been struck. It could not be confirmed officially because Borussia Dortmund would not let him leave until they had played a European Champions League game with Parma.

Hard though Celtic tried, the German club were adamant that Lambert's presence was essential. The fans in the Westfalenstadion took a similar view of his worth. After the 2–0 victory over Parma, there were extraordinary scenes as the midfielder lapped the stadium while he and the crowd said an emotional goodbye to one another. Few British players have been held in such esteem at a foreign club and the mere fact of Lambert's presence in Dortmund was uncanny.

Although he had been captain of the Scotland side that progressed to the semi-finals of the under-21 European Championship in 1992, it appeared that Lambert was set for an honourable but mundane career. The settings in which he found himself sometimes concealed his merits. He had moved from St Mirren to Motherwell and was occasionally embroiled in the struggle just to survive in the Premier Division.

Nonetheless, his abilities had always been present, even if it took a sharp eye to detect them. In September 1994, Motherwell lost 3–0 at home to Borussia Dortmund in the UEFA Cup. Ottmar Hitzfeld, the coach of the visiting side, noted the manner in which Lambert had maintained the quality of his performance even while the match was collapsing around his ears. Other factors also encouraged Dortmund.

Celtic thought of buying Lambert in the summer of 1996, but would have had to pay a fee to Motherwell. No such considerations affected Dortmund.

Following the Bosman ruling, a player who was out of contract could move between countries for nothing. This particular free agent was to prove precious. The German club devised a position for Lambert in front of the defence, where his intelligence allowed him to intercept and his dependable passing provided the basis of counter-attacks.

European Cup glory

Dortmund have a working-class support who felt an affection for a player who had come straight from the comparatively humble background of Motherwell, but their approval rested on far more than sentiment. Lambert, in his first season in Germany, won the European Cup, after a 3–1 victory over Juventus in the Final. And it was from his cross that Karlheinz Riedle opened the scoring.

Paul LAMBERT	
Born: August 7, 1969	
Birthplace: Glasgow	
Height: 5ft 11in.	
Weight: 9st. 10lb	
Age: 28	
Position: midfielder	
Club record:	
St Mirren, Motherwell, Borussia Dortmund, Celtic	
International record:	
9 caps, 0 goals	
Scotland debut:	
vs. Japan, May 21, 1995 (0–0 draw)	

Paul Lambert raises the European Cup aloft after the 3–1 victory over Juventus in Munich in 1997

Berti Vogts has even said that he wishes Lambert were German so that he could pick him for his own team. Scotland have become increasingly grateful for the midfielder's nationality.

He made his debut for his country against Japan in 1995, while still a Motherwell player, but the year at Dortmund has refined his talent. Even the rigour of training in Germany came as a shock. In Britain, jokes and the sort of fun that sees the goalkeeper play centre-forward are part of a tradition.

Such events would be unthinkable at Dortmund. So seriously are practice matches conducted that, according to Lambert, the teams even use the off-side trap. More than the culture of the club, however, may have been the company he was keeping that saw Lambert develop. It must surely be stimulating to work beside men such as Matthias Sammer and Andy Möller.

Lambert keeps a cool head even in the heat of battle

Lambert performed with distinction for Scotland, first securing widespread acclaim when he shut Andreas Herzog out of the action during the 2–0 win over Austria in April 1997. All the same, he cannot be portrayed simply as a bouncer who refuses opponents access to the penalty area. The midfielder is prized because he is also capable of valuable creative work.

At Pittodrie, his chip, with its impeccable back-spin, gave Kevin Gallacher the chance to put Scotland 3–1 ahead against Belarus. Consecutive matches for Celtic in January 1998 saw him score a 25-yarder against Rangers and a 35-yarder against Motherwell. The Premier Division has been enhanced by his return, even if it seemed perplexing that Lambert should give up his life in Germany, where his day at the club started with a game of head tennis against Möller.

His lifestyle had few blemishes either, for he stayed in the house that used to belong to Patrik Berger. Despite the apparently idyllic conditions, it proved difficult for his wife and son to settle in Dortmund when Lambert was so often away from home. He had, for example, to spend a month in a training camp in Portugal during the winter shutdown.

The midfielder may have returned to Scotland, but with the World Cup ahead, he is certainly not in retreat.

Jim **Leighton**

In Scotland's game against Estonia at Rugby Park, Kilmarnock, in March 1997, Jim Leighton had the last touch of the afternoon, diverting Meelis Rooba's shot around the post.

It was a spry save and the applause cascaded from the stands. If the goalkeeper had heard it at all, he would probably have tried to block up his ears. Leighton was absorbed in dissatisfaction with himself, testily shaking his head and evidently angry that he had not held on to the shot. After all these years, the assault on perfection continues.

Perhaps that intensity is the key to his football longevity. He will be 40 in July, but is no nearer declaring a truce with any little failings that he possesses. Jim Leighton is as thin as a filament and a powerful current runs through him. Although there have been some hardships for him in the game, we ought to note how he has forced football to compensate him for the distress he once suffered. Leighton might still feel the odd twinge, but the disappointments are distant.

The story has been told so many times. Leighton was one of the key influences in the Aberdeen side of Alex Ferguson that dominated Scottish football and won the Cup-Winners' Cup in 1983.

Then came Manchester United, where he shared in some hesitant years at Old Trafford and was dropped by Ferguson for the replay of the 1990 FA Cup Final, just when the club was going to win a trophy. There was further despondency, with Dundee, and it seemed that all the lights in his career had been switched off.

Only a move to Hibernian in 1993 hauled him out of the darkness. He received assistance at the Edinburgh club, whose manager of the time, Alex Miller, is now his boss at Aberdeen, but the restlessness in Leighton's heart must have been his greatest asset. The glory days at Pittodrie in the early 1980s

Jim Leighton's career could have ended but he has recovered to make his presence more forcibly felt

Jim LEIGHTON

Born: July 24, 1958
Birthplace: Johnstone
Height: 6ft
Weight: 13st. 6lb
Age: 39
Position: Goalkeeper
Club record:
    Aberdeen, Manchester United, Dundee, Hibernian, Aberdeen
International record:
    83 caps, 0 goals
Scotland debut:
    vs. East Germany, October 13, 1982 (2–0 victory)

would not suffice and a yearning remained to be a success once more. A complete regeneration has been accomplished and Andy Goram's misfortunes with injury have allowed Leighton to enter a new era of heroics with the national team.

On the run-in to Euro 96, he started the last six matches and kept a clean sheet in them all. Seven appearances during the qualifiers for the 1998 World Cup did see him concede three goals, but he was still flawless. The display he produced in the 1–0 defeat of Sweden at Ibrox left the nation so much in his debt that it really ought to file for bankruptcy. None of these feats, however, puts Leighton entirely at ease. Despite his exploits before Euro 96, he found himself replaced by Andy Goram for the finals in England.

The two men share an excellence in their work, but in personality they have little else in common. Where football is concerned, Goram looks imperturbable. Leighton, on the other hand, cannot conceal his feelings and, after Euro 96, had considered retirement from the Scotland team.

First choice at last

His decision to press on, however, was rewarded in September of 1997 when, with both goalkeepers fit, Leighton was preferred for the match against Belarus at Pittodrie. It was the first time in seven years that Leighton could truly have claimed to be first choice for his country. At the 1990 World Cup in Italy, Scotland had stood by him despite his demotion at Manchester United and the goalkeeper appeared to be rebuilding his form.

Then, with nine minutes of the final group match against Brazil remaining, he could not quite hang on to a shot and Muller slipped the loose ball home for the only goal. For Leighton, who had been so close to vindication, it was a brutal blow.

An appearance against the same country in the

The veteran has learned to find joy in each important occasion for which he is picked

opening match of the 1998 World Cup, before the immense global television audience, would be the ultimate demonstration that he has been too strong to be buckled by adversity. All the same, there are no guarantees that he will take part in that game. He and Goram still appear to be vying for the position. Leighton regards himself as the representative of an earlier epoch and recalls that there were no specialist goalkeeping coaches around when he was learning his trade.

Leighton is largely self-taught, having instructed himself through the mistakes he made when he came into the Aberdeen team at the age of 20. He reflects that he does not possess the technical perfection of Goram, but that is just one more disadvantage he has overcome. Nowadays, at the important games, friends who kept the vigil with him as they waited for the wretched years to end are always present, sharing in the achievement.

They may all have a few more outings to come.

Gary McAllister

When Branco was around to take free-kicks for Brazil, there ought to have been signs up insisting on safety helmets and protective clothing for the defensive wall. At Italia 90, he thundered the ball against the head of Murdo MacLeod. Whenever people remind him of the vicious power of that shot, MacLeod, to this day, replies, "So they tell me." The player had to be brought round and although he tried to continue it became clear that he was still suffering badly. Substitution was unavoidable.

It looked as if Gary McAllister's moment had come. He was warming up on the sidelines and, as a midfielder, was the obvious replacement. It came as a surprise, therefore, when Andy Roxburgh, the coach, decided to reshuffle the team and bring on a defender, Gary Gillespie, instead. McAllister was a little disappointed, but a 25-year-old does not recognize how fleeting an opportunity can be and how long it might take to come round again.

Since that day, he has won many more caps, become captain of Scotland, earned a reputation as a footballer of refinement and collected a League championship medal with Leeds United. Only one task remained to be completed. This year brought McAllister his last chance to appear in the World Cup Finals and he clung to his status as a Scotland player in the face of all threats until a knee injury ended his hopes.

Just before he won his 50th cap, against Sweden in April 1997, he spoke as a man who was far more concerned with the days to come than the landmark he had reached. The possible relegation of his club, Coventry City, was alarming for its own sake but it also troubled him because of the consequences for his prospects.

"If Coventry can keep their Premier Division status then I think I'll be able to keep going," he said. "You've got to be playing at a high level every week if you want to continue in international football."

McAllister was a bit like a partygoer who arrived late and then showed no inclination to leave. He was 25 before he collected his first cap and if the start of his involvement was delayed then he was intent on ensuring that so, too, should be its conclusion.

Some of that tenacity was evident in the last of Scotland's World Cup qualifiers. A win was essential and that created an anxiety disproportionate to the actual threat of the Latvians.

Gary McAllister has always had a natural maturity that marks him out as a leader of teams

Gary McALLISTER

Born: December 25, 1964
Birthplace: Motherwell
Height: 5ft 10in.
Weight: 10st 11lb
Position: Midfielder
Age: 33
Club record:
Motherwell, Leicester City,
Leeds United, Coventry City
International record:
56 caps, 5 goals
Scotland debut:
vs. East Germany, April 25,
1990 (1–0 defeat)

With 66 minutes gone, Scotland were still only 1–0 ahead and the nerves shrieked when Andrejs Stolcers appeared to be moving into a dangerous position. McAllister had read the situation, followed the opponent's run and got himself into position to make a fine tackle.

Craig Brown values the intelligence of his captain's interpretation of a game, which is generally used in an attacking sense as he builds the moves. Over the years, some people may have begun to take McAllister for granted, but the Scotland manager prizes him as highly as ever.

The midfielder had serious trouble with his knee this season, but had his fitness been established he would have remained central to Brown's plans for the World Cup. McAllister, with his head held high, surveys a scene carefully and his adroit passing makes him capable of taking advantage of it.

Natural leader

His abilities receive respect from team-mates, but the midfielder's sturdy personality also makes him a leader. He failed to convert an important penalty against England in Euro 96 and was disconsolate.

"I know there are far more important things in life than football," he said, "but if you cut me open and had a look inside right now it wouldn't be a pretty sight. I don't know if I can sink any lower."

A year later, however, he was still forthright enough to take the penalty in Minsk that defeated Belarus. There is something slightly detached about McAllister that encourages others to follow him.

"Getting along with just myself for company has never been a problem," he once said, "so it wasn't that hard to leave Motherwell when I was 20 to come to England to join Leicester City."

Others in the Scotland squad find in him a comforting maturity and the nature of his life may have brought McAllister to an early adulthood. The

McAllister has cruelly been denied his chance to appear in the World Cup finals

death of his mother when he was only eight forced him to take on responsibilities.

"It's not that I was home alone as a child," he said, "but I did have a younger brother to look after when my dad was away."

In that youth, McAllister remembers collecting beer mats depicting members of the Scotland squad for the 1978 World Cup. Without him, the team that plays in France will still bear the imprint of his character.

Ally **McCoist**

After coming on as a substitute for Scotland and scoring the winner in the match with Greece in 1995, Ally McCoist was sorely tempted to celebrate by crawling into the advertising hoardings behind the goal and making his way from one corner flag to the other.

The Rangers forward has always known how to be distinctive, even if the thought of the referee's reaction did subdue him on that particular occasion. Sharp of mind and quick of riposte, a mere game has difficulty containing him.

Recently, McCoist has become the co-presenter of a television chat show in Scotland, having already taken his seat as one of the captains on the BBC's "A Question of Sport". No wonder Walter Smith, the manager at Ibrox, makes mock apologies for any intrusions that Rangers might make into McCoist's burgeoning media schedule. Even so, the joke should not be taken too far. The position of TV celebrity must appeal, but it still will not afford him the thrill that he finds in football.

Although he is 35 and knows there will be a great deal to occupy him for the rest of his days, McCoist is still attempting to thwart the injuries that would force him to retire from football. Craig Brown must have felt uneasy at the beginning of the year when he heard that the forward would have to rest his knee for a couple of months. There is plenty of good will towards McCoist, but Brown's reasons for wanting him back are entirely selfish.

There is a brazen streak to the player which somehow puts him at the forefront. You would cringe at the clichés of his career if it were not

For Ally McCoist, football often looks like a long burst of jubilation

Ally McCOIST

Born: September 24, 1962
Birthplace: Bellshill
Height: 5ft 10in.
Weight: 12st.
Position: Forward
Age: 35
Club record:
St Johnstone,
Sunderland, Rangers
International record:
59 caps, 19 goals
Scotland debut:
vs. Holland, April 29, 1986
(0–0 draw)

for the fact that they are so fascinating to witness. Who else could break his leg and then score the first goal of his comeback by trotting on as a substitute to deliver the winner in the 1993 League Cup Final with an overhead kick? Nobody is ever sure just how far his repertoire of the outrageous might extend.

Until Euro 96, he had never found the net in the finals of a major international tournament, but the man who is supposed to depend on penalty box poaching defeated Switzerland with a 20-yarder. Brown can hardly bear to dispense with so mercurial a figure and McCoist's general fitness is only of marginal concern. "We'll just stick him on a skateboard and shove him onto the pitch," the Scotland manager has sometimes joked.

Formidable charisma is not the striker's only gift. He has improved greatly as a player since the early days at Ibrox when the Rangers support would regularly boo him. Strength has been added and his first touch has grown more deft, but it is McCoist's sense of anticipation that has been enhanced most of all. He is rarely so solemn and dull as to comment on his own performance, but he does have one tale about a goal he scored from close range against Ayr United.

That evening a man in a pub sneered at the player for the easy pickings that had come his way in the game. "I could have got annoyed, but I just laughed," McCoist said. "He hadn't a clue about what had gone on in the five seconds before that had put me in position for the tap-in."

Game for a laugh

The forward is never likely to brood over such misunderstandings. McCoist is fuelled by his own high spirits and he could scarcely function at all if he tried to be earnest.

In the spell when former manager Graeme Souness was leaving him out of Rangers' starting line-up, McCoist one day took an inflatable cushion with him to the substitute's bench and began noisily to inflate it before sitting down. It was the act of a man who will not dwindle into dejection. On the pitch, too, he likes to banter with defenders, knowing that the repartee will often end with him having the last laugh as he claims a goal.

Jim Duffy recalls one match with Dundee when he was playing against the Rangers forward at Ibrox: "Ally scored early on, but we got an equalizer before half-time. I was quite pleased to be level at the interval and as we were going off I said to him, 'I'm glad you scored because I had your name in the sweep

Despite the injuries, McCoist has clung onto the hope of being in the 1998 World Cup squad

for the first goal.' Ally didn't even hesitate. He just replied, 'I hope you've got me for the second half as well because I'm going to score again.' Sure enough, he did."

Duffy also makes the point that defenders can lose their edge when marking McCoist because he can be such entertaining company. Scotland would like to be able to share in the McCoist merriment this summer.

Chapter 4
The Coach

At the end of last year Craig Brown sat beside a suave Glenn Hoddle, his England counterpart, in a BBC studio. "I reckon his suit cost more than my house," joked the Scotland manager. Brown presents himself as an ordinary person, the sort of man you could take for granted as a workmate or a next-door neighbour. He is approachable and at ease in every sort of company, but Brown is also much more than just a likeable bloke. A pleasant manner does not create the sort of record that he possesses.

When he became Scotland manager in 1993, following the resignation of Andy Roxburgh, there was some public unhappiness about the process. Brown had already been with the SFA for seven years, working as Roxburgh's assistant, and his promotion was rather low-key. Deep in our melodramatic hearts, most of us still hanker after a manager who is an impresario, or a witch doctor, or a general or, better still, all three.

Brown is not inclined to such theatrics. While others strain for effect, he, in fact, amounts to much more than he pretends to be. The low-key approach

has been successful, but it carried considerable risks.

He had attracted little interest when he started work in 1993 and so ensured that there was scarcely any pressure upon him, yet the absence of mystique also made him vulnerable. If results had been poor there would scarcely have been a murmur of dissent over his swift sacking. This, however, is a manager who was built to last.

New-boy Craig Brown is in gloomy mood as he sees Scotland lose 3–1 to Italy in October 1993

For a while, he was thought of as being, in outlook, Roxburgh's replica more than his heir. In itself, that would have been acceptable because Roxburgh was certainly a success in the job, but the partnership between the two men created misunderstandings.

The fact that they operated so well together did not mean that one was a psychological clone of the other. Brown, indeed, is a highly unusual individual. Strange though it may sound, this instantly identifiable Scotland manager with the affable manner is really a chameleon.

The range of his experiences allows him to fit in anywhere. When Andy Roxburgh was appointed in 1986, it was taken as a sign of a shift in philosophy by the SFA. Instead of bringing in a man from the rough and tumble of club football, they had given the post to someone with a background in the more rarefied practice of modern coaching. Brown straddles both categories. Unlike Roxburgh, he remained on the club scene long after his playing days were over. His time as a footballer is actually one of the briefer episodes in Brown's life.

Career cut short

He sometimes mocks his own abilities, but, in truth, nobody ever discovered how good he actually was. After signing for Rangers as a youngster, Brown damaged a knee and, with sports medicine barely in existence at the start of the 1960s, failed to recover fully.

In December of last year, he received confirmation that his left knee will have to be replaced with an artificial joint. Brown also played for Dundee and Falkirk, but, by his mid-20s, the injuries had ensured that there would be no further part for him to play on the field.

Following a spell as assistant manager of Motherwell, he went on to take charge of Clyde in 1977. Three of his players there – Steve Archibald, Pat Nevin and Ian Ferguson – would be involved in transfers worth £1m or more once they had moved to other clubs, but Clyde themselves were usually in penury.

Willie Dunn, the chairman of the time, was enough of a purist to have reservations about shirt sponsorship, until Brown explained that a deal with the British Oxygen Company would be worth £10,000. "Mr Manager," said Dunn solemnly, "for £10,000 I would be prepared to put B.O.C. on my bare chest."

Clyde was the right sort of place to get acquainted with the realities of football. Relegation had to be endured, but under Brown the club also collected two Second Division championships.

Just as important, his dealings in the transfer market assisted the finances. His time with Clyde also improved his understanding of the hurly-burly of the relationship with the fans. The club brought him on to the board and the following day, during an away game at Cappielow, a voice bellowed, "Hey Brown, now you're a director can you get us a decent manager?"

He loves to tell, too, of one visit to a supporters' club in Castlemilk. "Half of them were booing and half of them were cheering," the droll Brown recalls, "and the only problem was that the half that were cheering were cheering the half that were booing."

He was capable of dishing out some disparagement himself. One of his players who had scored and then been sent off for a piece of spectacular folly expected a tirade in the dressing room. The manager used only a single sentence: "Your father was a joiner and he made your head."

Controlling the emotions

Brown was young enough then to commit indiscretions. Gripped by a sense of injustice during a game

Craig Brown tries to avoid the extreme emotions that distort judgment

with Forfar, he marched on to the field at Station Park. Only once he was there did he recover full consciousness and realize just what he was doing. Nonetheless, he still stifled any sense of irony and accused the referee of losing control.

The episode is especially amusing because it does not accord with the impression we now have of Brown. He can be eerily calm before even the most tense of matches and you almost feel it would be possible to pass the time of day with him in the seconds before kick-off.

Few other managers are capable of preventing the frenzy from seeping into them. That temperament, though, is not an inherent part of the nature. As the Station Park anecdote suggests, he has had to labour to turn himself into the unflappable person with whom we have become so familiar.

He continues to be at home with the banter and gossip of the game in Scotland and he has his intricate web of friends and contacts, yet Brown is to be found in many other settings as well. After he had stopped playing, Brown had some experience of journalism and while employed in his part-time capacity at Clyde he earned his living by working as a college lecturer. At present, he holds an honorary position at Paisley University and occasionally appears there to give talks on topics such as management techniques. In Brown's character, hearty good humour co-exists with an academic strain.

Spymaster General

He is accepted by the sophisticates of the coaching scene and, like a prominent university professor, drifts through the circuit of lectures and seminars. Some of his acquaintances are illustrious and, on his trips to watch games in Germany's Bundesliga, the national coach, Berti Vogts, always insists on picking him up at the airport.

International football, with its insistence on intelligence and preparation, suits him perfectly. Brown has long enjoyed its subterfuge. He was part of the backroom staff taken to the 1986 World Cup by Alex Ferguson and discovered the lengths to which rivals will go in their attempts to gain even the smallest advantage.

Scotland sought to obtain some measure of privacy for a particular training session, but that only inspired others to try their hand at espionage. Vogts, who was

Despite experiencing the crowd's antagonism, Brown has a strong bond with Scotland's fans

then one of his country's coaching staff, first talked a drinks vendor into handing over his bib in return for a West Germany top and then donned the disguise in the hope that he could watch the Scots at work without being detected. As far as anyone knows, Brown has not yet resorted to that sort of ruse, but experiences in Mexico provoked him to thought and the consequences are still felt in the way he now runs the national team.

Brown's own respiratory system probably told him that there was something amiss in Scotland's operations. The 22 players taken to a tournament usually include three goalkeepers and once injuries start to occur it can become difficult to organize a full-scale practice match. At the 1986 World Cup in the broiling Mexican heat, he and others such as Walter Smith, the

Alex Ferguson introduced Brown to the international scene at the 1986 World Cup

Rangers manager until July 1998, had to play to make up the numbers, even though they were past the age when they could participate satisfactorily. Since then, Roxburgh and then Brown have always brought along half-a-dozen of the most promising teenagers.

With them around, it is always easy to have an 11-a-side game. Just as importantly, these youngsters are introduced to the ways of international football and given a glimpse of a possible future. If nothing else, it ought to fire their ambition. In the period influenced by Brown and Roxburgh, much of the work has been like that.

There are no grandiose schemes, just a steady reflection on events and the shrewdness to make small but important changes. Brown, with only four defeats in competitive matches since 1993, has a handsome record, but, like a mosaic, it is made up of many tiny pieces. The sequence of success is an accumulation of good decisions.

Attention to detail

For Brown, Germany are the ideal football nation because they are able to combine order with talent. He was beguiled by the sort of precision that was on show when Bayern Munich came to Glasgow for the 1976 European Cup Final with Saint-Etienne. Brown went to watch them train at Somerset Park in Ayr and saw the squad emerge from the tunnel impeccably dressed in either black tops or white. Without a word from Dettmar Cramer, the Bayern coach, the players broke into groups and went ahead with games of five men against two in different corners of the pitch. All the different phases of training were executed perfectly with virtually no need for instructions.

When a strategy is correct and carried out with flawless concentration a team becomes formidable. The inclination of the Scotland staff to pore over videos and to compile dossiers is sometimes dismissed as being pedantic, but just one thing learned can have great repercussions.

During a match with France at Hampden in March 1989, when Brown was still Roxburgh's assistant, Scotland led 1–0, but it was far from certain that they could hold the opposition at bay. Watching the videos, the coaches had noticed that central defender Luc Sonor was not reliable on his left foot and, before the game, the players were told to be ready to pounce on this weakness when he was attempting to play the ball on that side.

Sonor duly made a mistake and lost possession. Steve Nicol whipped in a cross from the right and Maurice Johnston's header increased the lead, putting the game beyond France's reach. It was that fixture, above all, that eased Scotland through to the 1990 World Cup finals and the victory owed much to minute attention to detail.

The national team, in all candour, does not possess the sort of brimming imagination that would allow it to improvise its way to success. Scotland depend on deliberation in the build-up and attentiveness during the game itself.

Playing to the strengths

In his preference for a 3–5–2 formation, Brown differs radically from Roxburgh, who was more of a 4–4–2 kind of coach.

Andy Roxburgh worked closely with Brown, but their ideas differ

The tactics that Brown has adopted are, in part, the result of pragmatism because they let him play as many as possible of the several excellent centre-backs that Scotland possess.

Even so, every system has its inherent frailties and 3–5–2, in theory at least, should leave a team with only a single player to cover on each wing. Brown came up with his own way of compensating for the weakness. In contravention of orthodox practice, two of the centre-backs stand on the outside of the forward they are marking. Therefore, if the ball is pushed wide, they have a head start and should be able to reach it first, and if the opposition tries to pass straight through the middle, the third centre-back is still there to make the interception.

The approach is slightly unconventional and Brown has also faced up to the difficulties of instilling ideas which players do not encounter at their clubs. A lack of available time with the squad makes the task even more awkward. His men often arrive for international service weary or carrying slight injuries, and there might only be one proper session in which to work with them.

It is Brown's habit, with the help of the technician Brian Hendry, to use videotape to tutor players. They can be shown on screen, if not on the training ground, the positions that they are meant to take up at each situation. Diagrams are put on a projector, too, and printouts of them are pinned up on the dressing room walls at the match itself. The purpose is always to relieve players of anxiety.

Matt Elliott, the Leicester City defender, made his debut as a substitute in the friendly with France in November and while he waited and waited on the touch-line there must have been a fear that nervousness would wipe the instructions from his mind. Elliott knew, though, that there was a refresher course available on the dressing room wall.

Over the years, Brown has assembled his own way of doing things. He has a restless intelligence and continues to look for refinements. Despite a sociable disposition, Brown will confess to rather enjoying the long car journeys to games when he is alone and can turn matters over in his mind.

Taking the fizz out of life

Even his experiences on holiday may be put to use. In 1997 a friend invited him out to Hong Kong and while there he chatted to racehorse trainers who will not give the animals so much as a sweet. Brown was told that the principle is, "Don't contaminate the food supply." It led to him taking advice on the catering for the Scotland squad and fizzy drinks are now banned. Even a sparkling mineral water is off limits.

When dishing out the orders to the players, Brown told them that he had got it all from a horse doctor. That comment was probably intended to tease. It does no harm to deflate any vanity that might lurk within his stars by reminding them that they might be regarded in the same way as the four-legged thoroughbreds.

In reality, the squad can expect to be treated with consideration. They deserve it and, in any case, the old-fashioned style of hectoring is obsolete nowadays when dressing rooms contain affluent men who need not fear for the future. Mutual respect makes more sense than intimidation.

Brown is a reasonable man and he is quick-witted enough to find a diplomatic answer that allows him to evade controversy. The urge towards conciliation runs deep, but there are occasions when he concludes that particular steps must be taken and then he becomes implacable.

Best team does not equal best players

The most-publicized case involved Richard Gough. After Gough criticized the Scottish coaches in 1993 he was not picked for the squad. Although strenuous campaigns for the defender's reinstatement followed, Brown would not be swayed. "It's your duty to pick the best players," he was told. "No it's not," said the manager, "It's my duty to pick the best team."

The Gough issue was extremely unusual, but Brown recognizes that ruthlessness is one of a manager's obligations. His sincere loyalty to players who have been effective does have its limits. Of the squad that travelled to the European Championship in 1996 there may, at a guess, be nine players who are not chosen to go to France.

The exercise of tact does not prevent him, when necessary, from removing familiar faces so that there is scope for newcomers to develop. He bears in mind the disasters that have befallen predecessors who continued, out of sentiment or habit, to select individuals who were well past their best.

A manager has to take charge. As Brown keeps on saying, he must act rather than react. Despite a taste for self-deprecation, Brown has a very strong sense of his own value and is confident enough to take an initiative that will be unpopular. Relationships with the Press are cordial, but no one can claim any longer, as they did in bygone decades, that newspapers pick the team.

"If you guys push me over the edge," Brown said to some journalists during one furore, "I'll just land on the first tee and knock my drive 250 yards down the middle." The image, although picturesque, was a reminder that he expects to come out on top.

Events have validated his opinions often enough. He, for example, was able to see the worth of Colin Calderwood and gave him his debut, at the age of 30, when few others could have visualized the player as an international centre-half.

Brown has a habit of unearthing older footballers who have toiled at unfashionable clubs and are ready to make supreme efforts when the astonishing chance comes to play for Scotland. Whatever conclusions Brown draws will be inspected and debated throughout the country. The manager, in turn, is under some unspoken obligation to keep in touch with every corner of the land.

Brown's control of the squad is firm despite his amiable manner

Manager and missionary

Brown's diary for December 1997 might, in its list of public engagements, have been mistaken for that of a particularly zealous member of the Royal Family. There are an extraordinary array of meetings with businessmen, foreign dignitaries, politicians, and schoolteachers.

It was not always so. Andy Beattie resigned as manager in June 1954 and was not replaced for almost four years. Despite having no particular individual in charge, Scotland still succeeded in qualifying for the 1958 World Cup finals. The absence of a manager is now inconceivable and claims that it should be a part-time position were dropped long ago.

The post has developed in such a way as to make Brown a football missionary to society at large. That December diary, which was published in *The Sun* newspaper, illustrates the manner in which his duties ripple outwards. Some activities, such as visits to matches or the trips to France for the World Cup draw and for the inspection of hotels that might be used at the tournament, were strictly concerned with the national team.

After that came the engagements when he represented the game in general. One day found him at a fund-raising event in Dundee for the St Joseph's junior side and soon afterwards he was in London for a BBC chat show.

Brown must also serve as a symbol for sport as a whole and so he helps launch a government health and fitness programme. Last of all, he functions as a figure in the general life of the nation. Could he ever have guessed, while being heckled at Clyde, that he would one day be helping the Royal Mail by supporting their 'post early for Christmas' campaign?

Surely he would not have complained had he been told that he would be engaged in the journey to a boys' club on Islay, with a tour of a distillery on the island included. In as many ways as possible he must bring himself into the life of the community.

While in the Highlands to open local side Deveronvale's new ground, Brown was introduced to a blind man called Albert Smith, who gave him the tip of his white stick so that he could have it as a good-luck token in France this year. In all his travels, the manager senses the deep love of the Scotland team that came into being at the end of the last century and has never faded since.

All this leaves Brown with a dizzying sense of obligation, but the emotions of the nation could not be in better hands.

CRAIG BROWN'S RECORD

Date	Tournament	Result	Venue
*October 13, 1993	(WC)	Italy 3, Scotland 1	Rome
November 17, 1993	(WC)	Malta 0, Scotland 2	Valletta
March 23, 1994	(F)	Scotland 0, Holland 1	Hampden
April 20, 1994	(F)	Austria 1, Scotland 2	Vienna
May 27, 1994	(F)	Holland 3, Scotland 1	Utrecht
September 7, 1994	(EC)	Finland 0, Scotland 2	Helsinki
October 12, 1994	(EC)	Scotland 5, Faroe Islands 1	Hampden
November 16, 1994	(EC)	Scotland 1, Russia 1	Hampden
December 18, 1994	(EC)	Greece 1, Scotland 0	Athens
March 29, 1995	(EC)	Russia 0, Scotland 0	Moscow
April 26, 1995	(EC)	San Marino 0, Scotland 2	Serrevalle
May 21, 1995	(F)	Japan 0, Scotland 0	Hiroshima
May 24, 1995	(F)	Ecuador 1, Scotland 2	Toyama
June 7, 1995	(EC)	Faroe Islands 0, Scotland 2	Toftir
August 16, 1995	(EC)	Scotland 1, Greece 0	Hampden
September 6, 1995	(EC)	Scotland 1, Finland 0	Hampden
October 11, 1995	(F)	Sweden 2, Scotland 0	Stockholm
November 15, 1995	(EC)	Scotland 5, San Marino 0	Hampden
March 27, 1996	(F)	Scotland 1, Australia 0	Hampden
April 24, 1996	(F)	Denmark 2, Scotland 0	Copenhagen
May 26, 1996	(F)	USA 2, Scotland 1	New Britain
May 30, 1996	(F)	Colombia 1, Scotland 0	Miami
June 10, 1996	(EC)	Holland 0, Scotland 0	Villa Park
June 15, 1996	(EC)	England 2, Scotland 0	Wembley
June 18, 1996	(EC)	Scotland 1, Switzerland 0	Villa Park
August 31, 1996	(WC)	Austria 0, Scotland 0	Vienna
October 5, 1996	(WC)	Latvia 0, Scotland 2	Riga
November 10, 1996	(WC)	Scotland 1, Sweden 0	Ibrox
February 11, 1997	(WC)	Estonia 0, Scotland 0	Monaco
March 29, 1997	(WC)	Scotland 2, Estonia 0	Rugby Park
April 2, 1997	(WC)	Scotland 2, Austria 0	Celtic Park
April 30, 1997	(WC)	Sweden 2, Scotland 1	Gothenburg
May 27, 1997	(F)	Scotland 0, Wales 1	Rugby Park
June 1, 1997	(F)	Malta 2, Scotland 3	Valletta
June 8, 1997	(WC)	Belarus 0, Scotland 1	Minsk
September 7, 1997	(WC)	Scotland 4, Belarus 1	Pittodrie
October 11, 1997	(WC)	Scotland 2, Latvia 0	Celtic Park
November 12, 1997	(F)	France 2, Scotland 1	Saint-Etienne

*Brown was only caretaker manager for this match
(WC) = World Cup; (EC) = European Championship; (F) = Friendly

Brown's overall record, to the end of 1997, is:
Played 38, Won 20, Drawn 6, Lost 12.
In competitive matches, the record is more impressive:
Played 25, Won 16, Drawn 5, Lost 4.

Chapter 5

World Cup History

Before the Second World War, the ordinary football supporter in Scotland was, at best, dimly aware of the World Cup. Then, it was a tournament contested by foreigners in distant lands. Now, the competition is to be found at the centre of all our lives.

The World Cup, of course, was bound to take root in the imagination once the countries of the British Isles began to enter it. Television also induced sophistication when it brought us, in colour, the transfixing images of Pele and his marvellous team-mates winning the trophy in Mexico in 1970.

Football has become cosmopolitan and at some point at the beginning of the 1980s the realization dawned that victory over England in the annual fixture was no longer sport's ultimate prize. The bond with the World Cup has been established by the deeds of Scottish players and by the joy, sorrow or anger they have aroused in the rest of us. Scotland have discovered, at times, that they are bumbling apprentices when compared to the great, polished nations, but the heritage is still one in which we can all take pride.

The highlights have often come in the qualifiers, and Craig Brown's team has maintained a doughty tradition. Sweden were third in the World Cup in 1994, but they will not be at this year's tournament because Scotland finished ahead of them. Admittedly, there are also days that make you wince, as when the side lost to Costa Rica in 1990, and accounts of the inept approach adopted in the 1950s are mortifying. After cringing a little, Scotland have tried to learn from even their most preposterous experiences.

Recognition grew of the complexity of a World Cup. This country, with its small population, has to husband resources, but managers are now acutely

Billy Bremner gives the Brazilians a taste of their own medicine during the 1974 World Cup Finals

Fred Martin cannot prevent the first goal in the 7–0 trouncing that traumatised Scotland in 1954

aware of the delicate assessment required when deciding which valued players have simply become too old to be of service. Misjudgement of that question hurt Scotland at tournaments in the 1970s and 1980s. Craig Brown knows that he will need to come up with a long series of correct answers if the team are to march beyond the first round in 1998.

The old ignorance and arrogance are gone, but obsession remains. The recognition of the talents of other nations and the scale of the challenge they present has not daunted us. Scots have only been given even greater cause to rejoice when our national team at long last makes its mark at the World Cup finals.

SWITZERLAND 1954

A tale of under-preparation

Just before kick-off in Scotland's first match in the finals of the World Cup, Ernst Ockwirk, the captain of Austria, presented his opposite number with a pennant. Willie Cunningham, the Preston North End full-back, was discomfited, because he had nothing to hand over in return.

The episode typified a lack of preparation. However, in view of the events that followed in Switzerland, Scotland would have been grateful if it had always been so easy to suppress the evidence of their involvement.

The Home International championship then served as a qualifying group for the World Cup and in 1954 Scotland had finished as runners-up, behind England. This entitled them to a place in the finals and the SFA, having refused the invitation under similar circumstances four years earlier, decided that the moment had come to accept.

The change in policy stemmed from a deepening appreciation of the status that the World Cup would achieve. The fact that it was being held in Europe, for the first time since the Second World War, also made attendance far more convenient. Even so, the World Cup still did not hold the whole of Scotland in thrall.

Rangers declined to let any of their players participate, preferring to take them on a close season tour of America instead. Scotland, therefore, had to do without such men as their captain, George Young. The desultory attitude towards the tournament was not confined to Ibrox. Scotland had little appreciation of the extent of the resources required.

Innocents abroad

A provisional squad of 22 was named for the finals, but only 13 men, including a single goalkeeper, were taken to Switzerland. Andy Beattie, the Huddersfield Town manager, was in charge of Scotland that summer, but was unhappy with the traditional arrangement of that era which saw him working under a committee of selectors, composed of SFA officials, who were free to ignore his views when picking the team. He had threatened to resign before the squad even left for Switzerland.

There was a muddled feeling about most issues concerning the Scots. No training kit had been supplied and the players prepared for the World Cup games while wearing their club jerseys. Willie Fernie, the Celtic forward, complained that they "looked like liquorice allsorts". In addition to being aesthetically displeasing, the odd assortment of colours failed to foster feelings of unity and professionalism. Nor had Scotland ensured that they would give the best possible account of themselves.

Having lost 4–2 to England in April, there was an irrational but deeply-felt desire for change. Strenuous efforts were made to find a fresh team, but it was a callow one that was created. Of the 13 players chosen

for the World Cup, only Bobby Evans and George Hamilton had made even 10 appearances for Scotland, and anyway, Evans did not play in either match at the finals.

Scotland brought trouble upon themselves at a time when they were already bound to encounter many problems set by the opposition. Austria were an ageing side, but they had been lauded as the foremost nation in Europe only a few years earlier and Uruguay were the World Cup holders.

When Scotland lost to Austria in their opening match, the 1–0 margin of defeat was almost encouraging. Beattie's side had come close to an equalizer in the closing minutes. Before Scotland could contest their next game, however, the manager's disagreements with his employers came to a head and Beattie announced that he would be resigning the post after the World Cup.

1954 FINALS, SWITZERLAND

June 16, Zurich
Scotland 0 Austria 1 (Probst)
Scotland:
Martin, Cunningham, Aird, Docherty, Davidson, Cowie, McKenzie, Fernie, Mochan, Brown, Ormond.

June 19, Basle
Scotland 0 Uruguay 7 (Borges 3, Abbadie 2, Miguez 2)
Scotland:
Martin, Cunningham, Aird, Docherty, Davidson, Cowie, McKenzie, Fernie, Mochan, Brown, Ormond.

Pool 3 Final Table

	P	W	D	L	F	A	Pts
Uruguay	2	2	0	0	9	0	4
Austria	2	2	0	0	6	0	4
Czechoslovakia	2	0	0	2	0	7	0
Scotland	2	0	0	2	0	8	0

Meltdown

Few hopes remained and Vittorio Pozzo, the former Italy manager, foretold doom for Scotland against Uruguay with particular accuracy. "They will die in the sun," he said. Scotland had begun to falter even before the match began.

The Uruguayan national anthem that lasted some six minutes seemed of operatic duration to players who stood and sweated in the unrelenting 100-degree

Scotland seemed to be caught up in a perpetual goalmouth incident while being outplayed by Uruguay

heat of the day. Scotland felt the weight of their heavy jerseys and clumpy boots as they studied the stylish, modern garb of their opponents. Uruguay were fast and skilful, leaving Tommy Docherty, the midfielder who would one day become Scotland's manager, to joke that he and the rest of the side got sunburnt tongues from their panting pursuit of the South Americans.

They rarely caught them. In one of the most humiliating results ever endured by Scotland, Uruguay won 7–0. It is claimed that Beattie's player were so exhausted that they simply kept their strips on while standing under the showers at half-time.

The goals were almost welcome for the respite they brought exhausted players. According to Docherty, the game was disrupted while each scorer gave a brief interview to a radio station. It is as well that no-one wanted to speak to the Scots. Their first brush with the World Cup finals had left them lost for words.

SWEDEN 1958

Where the World Cup is concerned, it can seem, on the more depressing occasions, that the learning curve is too steep for the Scots. They look as if they are climbing, but then lose their grip and slither painfully down again. Nonetheless, the 1958 finals did constitute a small but definite advance.

Credit was even due for qualification alone, since Scotland had got the better of Spain and Switzerland to progress to the finals in Sweden. An element of common sense had also begun to emerge and Scotland took a full 22-man squad to the competition.

If they remained hobbled, it was partly because of the after-effects of a tragedy. Matt Busby had been appointed as part-time manager at the beginning of 1958, but in February he was badly injured in the Munich air disaster that killed 23 people, including eight of his Manchester United players.

The side that drew 1–1 with Yugoslavia in 1958 – Scotland's first point in the finals

At the World Cup finals, Scotland were under the supervision of their trainer, Dawson Walker, while team talks were conducted by Tommy Younger, the goalkeeper. Efforts to find a more suitable replacement for Busby ought to have been made, but the national team was starting to learn that the greatest obstacle in the tournament lay in the merits of the other nations.

Scotland faced Yugoslavia, Paraguay and France in 1958. If football was susceptible to the laws of arithmetic, the players would have been too frightened to leave the dressing room for their opening match. England had beaten Scotland 4–0 before a desolate Hampden crowd in April, but had then themselves been beaten 5–0 by Yugoslavia in Belgrade. That evidence suggested that Yugoslavia would prove brutally superior to Scotland in a World Cup match, but sport, luckily enough, does not operate in so rigorously logical a manner.

All the early signs had justified foreboding. Stewart Imlach, the left winger, pulled a muscle in the third minute, but, in the era before the introduction of substitutes, he had to continue as best he could. Three minutes later, Yugoslavia notched the opener through Petakovic. There might have been further goals before the interval as a tentative, insecure Scotland side found few means of even pestering their opponents. The second half, though, saw the Scots cast aside their diffidence. Jimmy Murray capitalized on an error to equalize and might have won the game. The Yugoslav goalkeeper dropped the ball into his own net, but the referee ruled that Jackie Mudie had fouled him.

Underestimating the opposition

Although Scotland acquired respectability with the result, they were soon to let it fritter away. Paraguay were an unknown quantity, but their feat in reaching the finals at the expense of Uruguay meant that they deserved to be treated cautiously. All the same, it did not look as if Scotland had any detailed knowledge of what to expect.

The mobility of the Paraguayans was a persistent cause of distress to players who had coped well with the more static nature of the game against Yugoslavia. The athleticism of the South Americans also made opponents look flimsy, and the 3–2 defeat left the Scots with more than just their feelings hurt.

A catalogue of injuries included Graham Leggat's broken wrist. Scotland, however, were to remember the game most of all for the harm that they did to themselves. Younger had a wretched afternoon in what turned out to be his final international. Aguero's shot went through his legs to open the scoring and although Leggatt equalized, Scotland fell behind once more when Younger could do no more than help

---

1958 FINALS, SWEDEN

June 8, Vasteras
Scotland 1 (Murray) Yugoslavia 1 (Petakovic)
Scotland:
Younger, Caldow, Hewie, Turnbull, Evans, Cowie, Leggat, Murray, Mudie, Collins, Imlach.

June 11, Norrkoping
Scotland 2 (Mudie, Collins) Paraguay 3 (Aguero 2, Parodi)
Scotland:
Younger, Parker, Caldow, Turnbull, Evans, Cowie, Leggat, Collins, Mudie, Robertson, Fernie.

June 15, Orebro
Scotland 1 (Baird) France 2 (Kopa, Fontaine)
Scotland:
Brown, Caldow, Hewie, Turnbull, Evans, Mackay, Collins, Murray, Mudie, Baird, Imlach.

Pool 2 Final Table

	P	W	D	L	F	A	Pts
France	3	2	0	1	11	7	4
Yugoslavia	3	1	2	0	7	6	4
Paraguay	3	1	1	1	9	12	3
Scotland	3	0	1	2	4	6	1

another drive by Aguero on its way into the net. Fifteen minutes from the end the goalkeeper fumbled a corner and Parodi put Paraguay 3–1 ahead. Bobby Collins' long-range goal was not enough to compensate for Scottish mistakes.

A huskier side was selected for the concluding match in the group, with Dave Mackay and Sammy Baird added to the line-up. Bill Brown made his international debut as Younger's replacement. The Dundee goalkeeper was already 26, but there was still sufficient time left for him to win 28 caps. He was one of those goalkeepers whose efficiency has a calming effect on every team-mate in the vicinity. Great doses of reassurance were needed against France, whom Scotland had to defeat if there were to be any possibility of a place in the quarter-finals.

France, to general surprise, prospered at the 1958 World Cup and their prowess depended on a combination in attack that proved too strong for several teams, including Scotland. Just Fontaine laid on the opener for Raymond Kopa and then claimed one for himself. Fontaine would go on to set the record for the finals by scoring 13 goals in Sweden. Jackie Mudie hit the post with a penalty kick and later Baird found the net to reduce France's lead to 2–1. Scotland lost the match by that minimal margin.

They were also left pondering the size of the gap that really separated them from the standards of Kopa and Fontaine.

WEST GERMANY 1974

The only undefeated team

Scotland really learned to appreciate the World Cup once they were deprived of it. The finals became an obsession all across the globe in a period when Scots were obliged to spectate rather than participate. Deliverance came at an unlikely moment and it was provided by an improbable leader.

Tommy Docherty had given up the national manager's job at the end of 1972, to take up the post at Manchester United. He was replaced by Willie Ormond, who had been splendid in his labours with St Johnstone, but had still to prove that he was equipped to cope with the celebrity status and scrutiny that comes to the man who runs the Scotland team.

He began work in 1973, the SFA's centenary year, and Ormond's first match in charge came on February

---

1974 FINALS, WEST GERMANY

June 14, Dortmund
Scotland 2 (Lorimer, Jordan) Zaire 0
Scotland:
Harvey, Jardine, McGrain, Bremner, Holton, Blackley, Dalglish (Hutchison), Hay, Lorimer, Jordan, Law.

June 18, Frankfurt
Scotland 0 Brazil 0
Scotland:
Harvey, Jardine, McGrain, Holton, Buchan, Bremner, Hay, Dalglish, Morgan, Jordan, Lorimer.

June 22, Frankfurt
Scotland 1 (Jordan) Yugoslavia 1 (Karasi)
Scotland:
Harvey, Jardine, McGrain, Holton, Buchan, Bremner, Dalglish (Hutchison), Hay, Morgan, Jordan, Lorimer.

Group 2 Final Table

	P	W	D	L	F	A	Pts
Yugoslavia	3	1	2	0	10	1	4
Brazil	3	1	2	0	3	0	4
Scotland	3	1	2	0	3	1	4
Zaire	3	0	0	3	0	14	0

14, in one of the special fixtures arranged to celebrate the ruling body's anniversary. England were the opponents at Hampden and the match proved to be a St Valentine's Day Massacre. The visitors adapted cleverly to the icy conditions and won 5–0. Ormond was no orator, but in a radio interview the following day he did observe that the result meant that he was no longer obliged to stick by the Scotland team that his

Not even Brazil's Jairzinho and Rivelino could shake Scotland at the 1974 World Cup

predecessor had built.

Jim Holton had just moved from Shrewsbury Town to Manchester United and was picked to play in an under-23 match against Wales in Swansea in March 1973. Ormond had a scout's eye for talent. He was in the market for replacements, so he watched Holton. Having seen the centre-half belt a clearance straight out of the ground and perpetrate some uncouth challenges, the legend goes that Ormond murmured, "He'll do."

Holton was to prove highly effective against even the most subtle forwards that Scotland encountered. Danny McGrain and Joe Jordan were among the others who made their debuts in the early months of Ormond's tenure. Results did not improve and five of the manager's first six games were lost.

Enver Maric, the Yugoslav goalkeeper, foils Joe Jordan in 1974

Unassuming though he was, Ormond never hesitated to back his own judgement and two more players, George Connelly and Tommy Hutchison, were actually given their debuts in one of the most important matches in Scotland's history, against Czechoslovakia in September 1973. Holton and Jordan, Ormond's discoveries, scored the goals in a tumultuous 2–1 victory that secured Scotland's place at the 1974 World Cup in West Germany.

Goal difference gloom

The performances there are the best Scotland have yet produced at the finals. The team was sturdy in defence and authoritative in midfield, where Billy Bremner and David Hay combined aggression with discriminating passing. Only a slight shortage of firepower in attack impeded Scotland's progress.

The team soon took a 2–0 lead against newcomers Zaire in the first match, with Peter Lorimer driving home a thunderous volley and Jordan glancing a header that bounced through the goalkeeper's legs, but the match was then disrupted when the floodlights failed and had to be repaired.

Bremner, as captain, has been faulted for the conservative approach he took in the remainder of the game, but Zaire were energetic and it is arrogant to assume that Scotland could have improved their goal average at will. Zaire were, admittedly, to concede nine to Yugoslavia, but Brazil could only beat them 3–0.

It was in their own match against Brazil that the greatest opportunity really slipped away from the Scots, who dominated the action but could not break the goalless deadlock. One half-chance broke off Bremner and rolled infuriatingly wide of the post.

Jimmy Johnstone, the great if maverick Celtic winger, was in the squad in Germany and had played supremely well in a 2–0 win over England the month before. He had only taken part on that occasion after being forgiven for a foolish escapade a few days earlier, when he had been pushed out into the Firth of Clyde in a rowing boat without oars. Another indiscretion was to follow in Norway, during the build-up to the World Cup finals, and this time forgiveness was not dispensed so readily.

The winger was not used in any of Scotland's matches in West Germany, even though his genius might have made all the difference in a very tight group. In the final game, Jordan hit a late equalizer to force a 1–1 draw with Yugoslavia, but Scotland were still eliminated from the tournament on goal difference. All the same, the players had acquitted themselves well and 10,000 people gathered at Glasgow Airport to greet the plane that brought them home.

West Germany, the eventual winners, lost to East Germany in a group match, and Scotland turned out to be the only undefeated team at the 1974 World Cup.

ARGENTINA 1978

Blinded by the hype

There is nothing quite so fascinating as a fiasco. An exhibition on the history of Scottish football was held in Glasgow in 1983 and there was a series of associated talks on all the glories of the game. The biggest audience, however, came not to relive triumphs, but to pick through the calamities of a World Cup campaign that had ended all of five years before.

Scotland, to this day, remains captivated by everything that occurred in Argentina in 1978. Miserable though the results were, it was a period when the relationship between the country and the team was at its most excitable.

Ally MacLeod, who had succeeded Willie Ormond as manager, has been lambasted over the events of that summer. In attacking him, though, supporters may really be berating themselves for their own gullibility. MacLeod was an astonishing showman and perhaps we ought to spare a moment to recollect the enjoyment he brought to the business of following Scotland. Only in his period could there have been serious discussion of the fantasy circulated by some supporters of hiring a submarine to take them to Argentina.

Asked what he proposed to do after the World Cup, MacLeod replied, "Retain it." The manager and the public, however, took the rhetoric all too seriously. There was a fabulous silliness about the willingness of a crowd of 25,000 to gather at Hampden, when there was no game to be played, so that they could wave goodbye to the players before the squad set off for South America.

In the emotional bedlam, reality was utterly drowned out yet we ought to have seen what was coming. Scotland had failed to win a match at the 1978 Home Internationals and had even been beaten by

England at Hampden. MacLeod possessed a squad that had been imposing a year earlier, but crucial elements had begun to wear out. Don Masson and Bruce Rioch, two excellent midfielders when in their prime, were in decline and had also become caught up in the general malaise at Derby County. The Scotland manager ignored the signs and stood by them even though he had several younger players who were capable of replacing them.

Argentina in 1978 was to be a tale of miscalculation. Virtually every decision, including the choice of hotel, turned into a topic of cantankerous debate.

From bad to worse

Scotland were hopelessly unprepared and brought to Argentina an injured player, Gordon McQueen, who did not make a single appearance. Only one left-back, Willie Donachie, was chosen for the squad and he was suspended for the first match in which Peru's right

Kenny Burns clears from Teofilo Cubillas, but the Peru forward got the better of Scotland in 1978

1978 FINALS, ARGENTINA

June 3, Cordoba
Scotland 1 (Jordan) Peru 3 (Cueto, Cubillas 2)

Scotland:
Rough, Burns, Kennedy, Forsyth, Buchan, Rioch (Macari), Masson (Gemmill), Hartford, Dalglish, Jordan, Johnston.

June 7, Cordoba
Scotland 1 (Eskandarian o.g.) Iran 1 (Danalfar)

Scotland:
Rough, Buchan (Forsyth), Jardine, Burns, Donachie, Macari, Gemmill, Hartford, Jordan, Dalglish (Harper), Robertson.

June 11, Mendoza
Scotland 3 (Dalglish, Gemmill 2 (1 pen.))
Holland 2 (Rensenbrink pen., Rep)

Scotland:
Rough, Donachie, Buchan, Kennedy, Forsyth, Rioch, Hartford, Gemmill, Souness, Dalglish, Jordan.

Group 4 Final Table

	P	W	D	L	F	A	Pts
Peru	3	2	1	0	7	2	5
Holland	3	1	1	1	5	3	3
Scotland	3	1	1	1	5	6	3
Iran	3	0	1	2	2	8	1

winger, Munante, took advantage of the situation to wreak havoc.

Although Scotland took the lead through Jordan, Cueto equalized. Masson then missed a penalty that would have restored the lead and Cubillas went on to score twice for Peru. The 3–1 defeat was followed by the revelation that winger Willie Johnston had failed a drugs test.

He had taken Reactivan pep pills that would have stimulated him no more than a cup of fresh coffee. But Reactivan contained a banned substance. Johnston had brought disgrace on Scotland and was immediately sent home.

The men who remained looked as if they were drained of all morale. Against the whipping boys of the group, Iran, they trudged through a 1–1 draw; their goal came only when Eskandarian turned the ball into his own net. Although Scotland had not lost, the result incurred even more wrath from supporters who made such extraordinary efforts to be in Argentina. The loathing and the humiliation had rarely been so extreme.

Scotland's response was one of defiance, even if they could not quite redeem themselves in the group. To reach the second phase, MacLeod's side needed to

Archie Gemmill en route to an unforgettable goal against Holland

beat Holland by three goals and came painfully close to doing so.

Amid all the anarchy, some reshaping of the Scotland side had occurred and although the midfield for the final game still featured Rioch it also included Archie Gemmill and Graeme Souness. Rob Rensenbrink opened the scoring, but Dalglish levelled the match and Gemmill, with a penalty, put Scotland in front. Gemmill then capped that with a goal that will survive in the nation's consciousness so long as there is a video recorder left to replay it.

Working his twisting way through a pack of defenders, the midfielder tucked the shot into the net with an impudent calm. Scotland were 3–1 ahead and on the verge of the extraordinary result they sought. Holland, however, quickly obliterated the dream when Johnny Rep bashed home a 25-yarder. That response by the Dutch revealed the mental toughness that would carry them all the way to the World Cup Final. Despite the warmth of that lone victory, Argentina was a chilling experience that continues to bring a shudder to Scottish hearts.

SPAIN 1982
Aberrations prove costly

After the upheavals of Argentina, Scotland needed a manager whose very name was a promise of professionalism. There was only one plausible candidate. Fortunately for Scotland, Jock Stein was available.

In August 1978, after 13 years of unparalleled success with Celtic, he left the club and became manager of Leeds United. Stein was not really at peace with the idea of constructing a new life in England, however, and ended his three-month stay at Elland Road by agreeing to succeed Ally MacLeod.

Stein had long been regarded as the ideal appointment, but the SFA were not alone in coveting him. Many clubs wished to prise him away from Celtic when he was at the height of his powers. He had, in fact, been manager of Scotland on a part-time basis for the last seven months of 1965. It had not been a wholly satisfactory arrangement and there was jubilation when Scotland at last obtained exclusive claim on his services.

By then, some of the extraordinary dynamism had ebbed away from Stein, who had been involved

in a dreadful car accident in July 1975. He was, all the same, the man who had created a revolution in Scottish football when making Celtic, in 1967, the first British club to win the European Cup.

His handling of players, his attention to detail and his tactical shrewdness were all of the highest calibre. No man has ever had better credentials to be manager of Scotland. His legacy is to be found in the meticulous detail with which the managers who have followed him now prepare the national team. In effect, Stein established a new tradition, curing Scotland of the stigma of amateurism.

1982 FINALS, SPAIN

June 15, Malaga
Scotland 5 (Dalglish, Wark 2, Robertson, Archibald)
New Zealand 2 (Sumner, Wooddin)
Scotland:
Rough, McGrain, F. Gray, Hansen, Evans, Souness, Strachan (Narey), Dalglish, Wark, Brazil (Archibald), Robertson.

June 18, Seville
Scotland 1 (Narey) Brazil 4 (Zico, Oscar, Eder, Falcao)
Scotland:
Rough, Narey, F. Gray, Souness, Hansen, Miller, Strachan (Dalglish), Hartford (McLeish), Archibald, Wark, Robertson.

June 22, Malaga
Scotland 2 (Jordan, Souness) USSR 2 (Chivadze, Shengelia)
Scotland:
Rough, Narey, F. Gray, Souness, Hansen, Miller, Strachan (McGrain), Archibald, Jordan (Brazil), Wark, Robertson.

Group 6 Final Table
	P	W	D	L	F	A	Pts
Brazil	3	3	0	0	10	2	6
Russia	3	1	1	1	6	4	3
Scotland	3	1	1	1	8	8	3
New Zealand	3	0	0	3	2	12	0

Not even forethought, though, could spare Stein the dread and the tension that come with the job. The qualifiers for the 1982 World Cup exacted the usual amount of distress and the 0–0 draw in Belfast, when Scotland believed that a point from the match was a necessity, was not for the squeamish.

With Kenny Dalglish, Joe Jordan, Graeme Souness, Willie Miller and Danny McGrain available to him, Stein did not lack experience or quality in the squad he took to Spain. The conundrum lay in the even greater resources possessed by the two principal rivals in the group, Brazil and the USSR.

Only against New Zealand was there the possibility of uncomplicated victory. Before that fixture, Scotland's first in the finals, Stein still employed his cunning to the full, talking incessantly about Jordan's power in the air. Any experienced Stein-watcher would have guessed what was to happen next.

Minnows bite back

Jordan was not in the team. New Zealand's defence, who had expected to tussle with him, were unprepared for the runs from deep positions which Scotland utilized. After Kenny Dalglish snapped up the first goal, John Wark, a midfielder, scored twice in the first-half.

The 3–0 lead was eroded when Scotland waned in the heat and the conditions were particularly savage in their impact on McGrain, the captain, who was not to start another match in the tournament. New Zealand found two goals of their own, before John Robertson and Steve Archibald restored Scottish composure with a goal apiece.

A 5–2 victory is always attractive, but with Brazil as their next opponents, Stein's side had needed to improve their goal difference to an even greater extent against New Zealand. This was a fine Brazil side with a midfield that gracefully filleted most opposition. The centre-forward, Serginho, was of a lesser calibre, but, against Scotland at least, Tele Santana's side were not brought face to face with the limitations of their

David Narey lashes home the goal that provoked Brazil in 1982

attack. Stein, if not precisely conceding defeat, had decided to conserve the squad's strength.

Dalglish, for example, was used only as a substitute. David Narey put Scotland in front with a wonderful 20-yard drive. The only problem with the goal was that it had been struck far too early in the game. Brazil went on to score four goals of their own. Not that it much mattered.

Scotland had long assumed that the group would be resolved with the match against the USSR. With victory essential – the USSR had the advantage of a better goal difference – Stein's side made an urgent start and, after a period of command in which the exuberant Strachan impressed, moved in front with Jordan's goal.

Scotland, however, had weakened in the second half of each of their matches in fiery Spain and did so again. The USSR got a muddled equalizer from Chivadze and an even more grotesque episode followed. Miller and Hansen collided while attempting to clear a harmless ball; Shengalia was left in possession and he took his chance slickly. Scotland regrouped and Souness' precise drive spared them defeat, but a 2–2 draw was insufficient.

Once again, the team had experienced the ruinous consequences of fleeting aberrations.

MEXICO 1986

One point, one goal and home

For Scotland in 1986, the World Cup finals in Mexico were an act of remembrance. It was impossible to watch the team that summer without recollections of Jock Stein welling up in your mind. He had died of a heart attack immediately after a match that went a long way toward ensuring qualification for the tournament. A draw with Wales in Cardiff on 10 September 1985 had been essential and the manager's acute judgement played a great part in the achievement of the result.

Davie Cooper, a deft and ingenious winger, was not used when he might have been submerged by the waves of energy that rolled over the pitch. Instead, the Rangers player was only brought on as a substitute when tiredness had taken the pace out of the game.

With Wales ahead through a Mark Hughes goal,

Scotland saw too little of Davie Cooper's gifts, but he made two appearances in the 1986 finals

Cooper replaced Gordon Strachan and at once began to elude defenders who had been far more comfortable when engaged purely in a trial of strength. Wales were pinned back and, ten minutes from the end, David Speedie hooked the ball forward and saw it blocked by the outstretched arm of David Phillips.

Cooper was left with a degree of responsibility that verged on the intolerable, but managed to govern his nerves, guiding the penalty kick past Neville Southall's left hand and just inside the post. At full-time, there were eruptions of delight among the thousands of Scots who had travelled to Cardiff, and none of them could have known that Stein had collapsed. The efforts to revive him failed and soon the fans in Wales and the world at large learned that one of the great figures in the history of sport, and in the history of Scotland, had died.

Football, of course, continued, but it felt almost absurd to tell the national team to proceed, undis-turbed, with its programme of matches. Alex Ferguson, who had been acting as Stein's assistant, was the man charged with the restoration of normality. In 1985, he was still manager of Aberdeen, the club he had led to victory over Real Madrid in the Cup-Winners' Cup final two years earlier.

Subsequently, he has presided over the rebirth of Manchester United as a great force in English and European football. In view of his impact over so long a period and on both sides of the border, it can be argued that he is a man to be ranked with Stein.

All the same, following Stein, in 1985, was a tormenting task. Ferguson assumed the duties while

---

1986 FINALS, MEXICO

June 4, Neza
Scotland 0 Denmark 1 (Elkjaer)
Scotland:
Leighton, Gough, Miller, McLeish, Malpas, Strachan (Bannon), Souness, Aitken, Nicol, Nicholas, Sturrock (McAvennie).

June 8, Queretaro
Scotland 1 (Strachan) West Germany 2 (Voller, Allofs)
Scotland:
Leighton, Gough, Miller, Narey, Malpas, Strachan, Souness, Aitken, Nicol (McAvennie), Archibald, Bannon (Cooper).

June 13, Neza
Scotland 0 Uruguay 0
Scotland:
Gough, Miller, Narey, Albiston, Strachan, McStay, Aitken, Nicol (Nicholas), Sharp, Sturrock (Cooper).

Group E Final Table

	P	W	D	L	F	A	Pts
Denmark	3	3	0	0	9	1	6
West Germany	3	1	1	1	3	4	3
Uruguay	3	0	2	1	2	7	2
Scotland	3	0	1	2	1	3	1

---

remaining manager of Aberdeen, and although he claimed at the time that he could cope with that double obligation he was later to acknowledge that he had submitted to an ordeal. Scotland dealt with the outstanding business readily enough.

As runners-up, behind Spain, in Group 7 of the qualifiers, they had to meet Australia in a play-off. A 2–0 victory at Hampden and a goalless draw in Melbourne allowed Scotland to become the 24th and last country to book their place at the 1986 World Cup finals.

Graeme Sharp's celebrations are misplaced. Fernando Alves' save kept the game with Uruguay goalless

Perishing in the "Group of Death"

Scotland are in danger of being accused of excessive whining over their bad luck in the tournament, but they had to be excused any small sigh that escaped from them upon learning that they would face Denmark, the 1984 European Championship semi-finalists, West Germany, two-time World Cup winners and 1982 runners-up, and uncompromising Uruguay, the 1983 South American champions. At least Ferguson's squad were not at risk from over-confidence, particularly once Kenny Dalglish had withdrawn with a knee injury.

Each of the games was gruelling and each turned away from Scotland. Charlie Nicholas was injured by a crude tackle in the match with Denmark and later Elkjaer took the break of the ball to score the only goal. The tactics were intriguing against West Germany, with Steve Archibald the sole striker as Scotland attempted to threaten with runs from midfield. Gordon Strachan scored and amused everybody by indicating that he was too small to vault the advertising

hoardings in celebration. But the Germans recovered to score twice and win.

For Scotland, the tournament came to a squalid conclusion against Uruguay, who had Batista, their full-back, sent off in the first minute for a foul on Strachan. The ten members of the side who remained whiled away the afternoon with time-wasting and more violent misdemeanours, for which FIFA imposed a fine of 25,000 Swiss francs. Scotland could not punish them, although Steve Nicol missed one fine chance. Yet again Scotland had sought a win and obtained only a draw.

The World Cup was proving as repetitive as it was infuriating.

ITALY 1990

Falling at the first hurdle

Scotland can claim to have exhausted every line of enquiry in seeking the answer to the problem of advancing the national team's status. Alex Ferguson's replacement, once he had stepped down, was Andy

Roxburgh, a man who had never gained a cap and never managed a club side.

His experience lay primarily in the 10 years he had spent as the SFA's director of coaching following his appointment in 1976. That was hardly the customary background and critics who dealt only in stereotypes mocked Roxburgh as a "schoolteacher". He had indeed worked in that profession, but it has never yet been explained why a gift for education should be thought worthless in football.

1990 FINALS, ITALY

June 11, Genoa
Scotland 0 Costa Rica 1 (Cayasso)

Scotland:
Leighton, Gough (McKimmie), McPherson, McLeish, Malpas, McStay, Aitken, McCall, Bett (McCoist), Johnston, McInally.

June 16, Genoa
Scotland 2 (McCall, Johnston pen.) Sweden 1 (Stromberg)

Scotland:
Leighton, McPherson, Levein, McLeish, Malpas, Aitken, MacLeod, McCall, Fleck (McCoist), Durie (McStay), Johnston.

June 20, Turin
Scotland 0 Brazil 1 (Muller)

Scotland:
Leighton, McKimmie, McPherson, Aitken, McLeish, Malpas, McCall, McStay, MacLeod (Gillespie), Johnston, McCoist (Fleck)

Group C Final Table

	P	W	D	L	F	A	Pts
Brazil	3	3	0	0	4	1	6
Costa Rica	3	2	0	1	3	2	4
Scotland	3	1	0	2	2	3	2
Sweden	3	0	0	3	3	6	0

Roxburgh, in fact, remains the only man to have steered a Scotland side to success in an international tournament of note. It was his team that won the European under-18 championship in 1982. Ernie Walker, Secretary of the SFA at the time, was therefore defiant whenever anyone tried to belittle Roxburgh following his appointment to the principal post in 1986, and called him "the best coach in the world". In 1998, with Roxburgh now employed as technical director for FIFA itself, Walker's opinion has some solid foundation.

Roxburgh served Scotland well, and most of the limitations of his seven years in charge of the national team were to be found in the talents of the men available to him. Good players continue to appear, but, strangely enough, the expertise of the recent crop has lain in defence.

Since the late 1980s there has been no midfield strategist to compare to Graeme Souness and the idea of a contemporary counterpart to Kenny Dalglish is no more than a pipedream. Under first Roxburgh and now Craig Brown, Scotland have become more professional than ever, but their need to be so is also greater than ever.

The degree of care shown in the build-up to a match, of course, does not prevent spontaneity and mass excitement from breaking when the real action begins. Scotland qualified for the 1990 World Cup finals mainly because of a night of delicious pandemonium at Hampden when France were beaten 2–0. The great Michel Platini, coach of the losing side, still believed that he possessed superior players and could not quite comprehend what had happened to them. Maurice Johnston was a significant part of the answer.

He scored both of the goals against France and amassed six in all during the qualifiers, a period in which he was playing for Nantes. Off the field, an on-off transfer to Celtic grabbed the headlines, but he was unaffected by the furore. Unluckily for Scotland, though, he could not remain detached from the processes of decline that apply to every footballer.

Costa Rica calamity

The national team has been prone to some bad timing at the World Cup finals. In 1978, Don Masson and

Juan Cayasso gives Costa Rica the lead and a dreadful day takes shape for Scotland in 1990

Maurice Johnston's penalty took Scotland to victory over Sweden on a stirring night in Genoa

Bruce Rioch were past their best. In 1982, Danny McGrain was only able to start the first match. In 1986, Souness was ruled out of the last game because Ferguson decided that his physical condition was not good enough. All were fine players, but Scotland's dependence on them extended beyond the limits of their own durability. The case of Johnston, who had joined Rangers in 1989, was less noteworthy, but at Italia 90, he was not the same predatory striker that he had been in the qualifiers. It was one factor that contributed to the ignominy of defeat by Costa Rica.

Scotland had a great deal of pressure but few real chances and Johnston, when given a sight of the target, was foiled by goalkeeper Conejo. Roxburgh's selection, which saw Alan McInally's height employed in attack, looked ill-judged. Costa Rica scored the only goal, when Jara's back-heel left Cayasso to finish.

Afterwards, as he faced some understandably indignant questioning, it was obvious that Roxburgh was only barely suppressing raw emotions. His squad must have been in similar condition for the match which followed, and it was one long out-pouring of Scottish passion.

The team used every legitimate means to claw at Sweden. The lead was gained when Stuart McCall turned home a corner kick and increased when Johnston converted a second-half penalty after Roy Aitken had been fouled. It took too long for Sweden to come to terms with the fury that Scotland had whipped up and they contrived only one late goal, from Stromberg.

It was an exhilarating night in Genoa. However, three points would not earn qualification for the second round and at least a draw, and more likely a victory, was required from the last game. Standing in the way of Scottish glory, however, were the group's top seeds and many people's idea of the eventual winners, Brazil. Sadly, Roxburgh's side were unable to duplicate the mood when they moved from Genoa to a rain-sodden match in Turin. They gave their all, but Brazil won 1–0, scoring through Müller in the 81st minute, after Leighton had been unable to hold on to a firm drive.

For the seventh time, Scotland had been knocked out in the first phase of the tournament. A place in the second round may sound like a humdrum attainment, but, for Scots, sheer elusiveness over a period of 44 years has turned it into a glittering prize

It all slipped away from Scotland when Brazil's Müller turned in the loose ball

THE ONES THAT GOT AWAY

Brazil 1950

Scotland has turned the self-inflicted wound into an art form, but this country's feat in knocking itself out of the 1950 World Cup must still be regarded as remarkable even by its own standards.

That was the first year in which there was a possibility of competing in a tournament which had begun in 1930. In common with the other footballing nations of Britain, Scotland had not previously been eligible to participate, having withdrawn from FIFA in the 1920s, and only returning to the fold in 1946.

FIFA, according a gracious welcome to these prodigal sons, announced that the 1950 Home International championship would serve as a qualifying group and that the top two teams in it could advance to that year's World Cup finals in Brazil. The SFA responded that they would only take part if they won the Home Internationals. To do so, it turned out, they required at least a draw with England, which would have given them a share of the championship.

Both countries found preparations uneasy, having been forced to stay outside Glasgow until shortly before the game because of an outbreak of smallpox in the city. During the match itself, Scotland remained troubled and lost 1–0 to a goal by Roy Bentley.

Willie Bauld came close to hauling the team level, but his shot struck the crossbar. Scotland were inches short of a draw, inches away from a place in the World Cup. Billy Wright, the England captain, asked George Young, his Scottish counterpart, to plead with the SFA for a change of stance.

Pride is inflexible and the SFA rejected all intercessions. Scotland took no part in the proceedings in Brazil. As news came back of England's defeat there by the USA, some may have concluded that Scotland's absence from the World Cup was a boon.

Chile 1962

By the beginning of the 1960s, the Scots were no longer aloof. Two appearances at the World Cup finals had been occasionally alarming, but also absorbing. Scotland now knew just how high the standards of international football were.

In their bid to reach the 1962 finals, they faced opposition from Czechoslovakia and the Republic of Ireland. The opening three fixtures were played in the first fortnight of May 1961 and a couple of victories over the Irish were efficiently harvested.

The 1960s produced a generation of outstanding players, who were thwarted at international level by defects of temperament and episodes of ill fortune. In 1961, Jim Baxter, Pat Crerand and Denis Law were among the crop of young men taking their place in the Scotland team. Unluckily for them, Czechoslovakia were vigorous and neat, if lacking in pace, and they possessed a great footballer in the midfielder Josef Masopust. Scotland lost 3–0 in Bratislava.

Even on their own turf, Scotland were often in distress. Czechoslovakia twice led at Hampden, but John White, of Tottenham Hotspur, set up three goals for Scotland. One was finished by Ian St John, the other two by the magnificent Law, whose winner came in the 83rd minute. Czechoslovakia then thrashed the Republic of Ireland twice and ended the group level on points with Scotland. Had goal difference applied they would have been easy winners.

Instead, there was a play-off in Brussels. Scotland were twice ahead through St John, but could never shake off the Czechs who were stronger in mind and body. The game went into extra-time before the Scots were beaten 4–2. Scotland had felt the full force of an excellent Czech team, and they proved just how good they were by advancing to the World Cup Final in Santiago, where they lost to Brazil.

England 1966

The 1966 World Cup was to be staged just across the border in England, but for Scotland it was a distant prospect. Their qualifying group was made up of minnows Finland, a capable Poland team and the intimidating Italians.

The matches with Finland were won and Scotland drew with Poland in Chorzow. The dreams began to unravel at Hampden, when Scotland, who were then managed by Jock Stein, led until the last few minutes before seeing Poland score twice to win.

The result left Scotland in the situation they had most dreaded, depending entirely on their results against the Italians. To be sure of finishing top of the group, Stein's side had to win both matches. That was an alarming assignment, particularly in a period when the Italian clubs were proving good enough to win the European Cup regularly.

For the game with Italy at Hampden in November 1965, Stein reinstated Jim Baxter, who had suffered a broken leg the year before. He also used Rangers' indomitable midfielder John Greig in the unfamiliar role of right-back.

The match possessed the expected character. Scotland pounded away but made few inroads and the Italians had a glint of menace on the counter-attack. Greig, who had scored the goal that won the game in Finland, was not the sort of person to resign himself to disappointment. With two minutes left, he came pounding through from the right, in a well-rehearsed move, to collect Baxter's

pass and drive the ball home. Scotland had beaten Italy 1–0. However, the chances of repeating the trick in the hostile atmosphere of Naples were poor.

Stein's squad was pulverized by injuries and, with few other options, he set out a defensive formation. The Italians were not to be kept at bay and won 3–0. Italy, as it turned out, had qualified only for the humiliation of defeat by North Korea in the finals and first-round elimination.

Mexico 1970

To those with a persecution complex, it sometimes seemed as if Europe was marshalling its greatest forces to bar Scotland's path. The West Germany of Franz Beckenbauer, Gerd Müller, Uwe Seeler, Sepp Maier and Berti Vogts were the implacable opposition in the qualifying group for the 1970 World Cup.

At least there were some matches of a therapeutic nature as well. After overcoming Austria 2–1 at Hampden, Scotland beat Cyprus 5–0 in Nicosia and 8–0 in Glasgow. Colin Stein, of Rangers, scored four goals in the home match but, since then, no Scotland forward has managed so much as a hat-trick.

Tom Boyd and Andy Egli level up, but Switzerland were clear winners in 1992

Between the recreational fixtures with Cyprus, West Germany had to be faced at Hampden in April 1969. For all their status as World Cup finalists of 1966, they had failed to beat Scotland on three previous occasions and manager Bobby Brown possessed players who could be formidable on their own territory. Such was the abundance of talent available to him that Bobby Murdoch, a consummate passer, was to be capped on only a dozen occasions. The match against West Germany was one of those appearances.

There was quality and bristling competitiveness in the match and the balance tilted towards the visitors when Gerd Müller, the arch-poacher, squirmed away from defenders to score. Scotland equalized with two minutes remaining when Charlie Cooke's subtlety opened up the space for the commanding Murdoch to run through and thunder home a drive.

His team was only deprived of victory in the last few seconds when Billy Bremner's attempt was cleared from the line by Beckenbauer. That contribution by the defender shaped the whole course of the group.

When Scotland travelled to Hamburg for their penultimate match, they could not afford to lose and, in practice, knew that even a draw would probably be inadequate. Yet another virtuoso of the 1960s, Leeds United winger Eddie Gray, helped Scotland into the lead with an elaborate run and shot that Maier could not hold, and Jimmy Johnstone netted the loose ball.

West Germany recovered to take the lead, but Alan Gilzean's header saw the pugnacious Scots draw level before Libuda clinched a 3–2 victory. Scotland had not deserved to lose and, once more, disappointment mingled with exasperation in the World Cup.

USA 1994

Unequivocal failure at least spares a side the torment of reviewing the what-might-have-beens. The qualifiers for the 1994 World Cup had scarcely begun before Scotland were attempting to salvage the situation.

After playing some thoughtful if unavailing football at the European Championship in 1992, Andy Roxburgh's team might have had too much faith in itself. Despite, or perhaps because of, an adventurous performance in Switzerland they lost 3–1.

Goalless draws with Portugal and Italy followed at Ibrox. In Lisbon, Scotland lost 5–0 to Portugal and Ally

McCoist broke his leg. After the 1–1 draw with Switzerland at Pittodrie, Roxburgh tendered his resignation and resisted all attempts to dissuade him.

Craig Brown, his assistant, acted as caretaker manager in a 3–1 defeat in Italy and was formally appointed to the post before a 2–0 win in Malta. Most people pitied him, believing that a long period of despondency was due after qualification for the World Cup finals on five consecutive occasions.

It is Brown's great achievement to have ensured that where his team is concerned pessimism is an aberration.

Despite all the exertion, Scotland's 1992 qualifier with Italy at Ibrox ended goalless

Chapter 6

Stars of the Past

They always tell you that football is a team game and so it is when you are watching a match and willing one side to victory. All the same, that is not how it feels afterwards. We relive the past by swapping anecdotes and recollections about the great players.

Down the decades, Scotland has been rich in individuals who seemed to be pursuing their own personal destiny. On occasions we groan about their waywardness and self-indulgence, but more often the country has been captivated by the mavericks, eccentrics and men who just happened to possess a superiority on the field.

In the time before the World Cup took hold, we measured players by their exploits against England. Scotland wore the primrose and pink racing colours of Lord Rosebery for the match at Celtic Park and the jauntiness found a delightful echo in R.S. McColl's hat-trick. The natural rivalry, nurtured by geography, has ensured that defeat of our English neighbours is a source of glee, and the 5–1 victory at Wembley in 1928 is enshrined in folklore because the diminutive forward line that triumphed through pure skill was the embodiment of all the Scottish daydreams.

Heroes against England

The members of that attack were extraordinary footballers. Alex James, with his raking passes, is sometimes credited as the man who turned Arsenal into an exalted institution. Alan Morton, of Rangers, was a lethal winger and so much the master of his art that he played on the left despite being naturally right-footed. Hughie Gallacher, a centre-forward of technique and instinct, was good enough to hold off vibrant rivals for the position. Celtic's Jimmy McGrory, for example, could score three goals in two games with England and still win only seven caps.

The late Billy Bremner was not always so courteous in his discussions with officials

Kenny Dalglish slickly fires in Joe Jordan's knock-down to score against Holland in 1978

One particular kick of the ball at Wembley, in 1936, was enough to ensure Tommy Walker the celebrity status that his accomplishment as a playmaker merited in any case. The 20-year-old had to take the penalty that offered Scotland a 1–1 draw and although the wind twice blew the ball off the spot, he converted it.

Sometimes it was not necessary to be a scorer to thrill the crowd. Jimmy Cowan, not long after recovering from a broken arm, became one of the few Scottish goalkeepers to conquer the citadel of the English. They called the 1949 match "Cowan's Wembley" and he was carried shoulder-high from the pitch following the 3–1 win.

The goalkeeper was abetted that day by George Young, a mighty defender who, despite his 15st. frame, was praised for lightness of foot. In the 1940s and 1950s, when international games were less frequent, the Rangers player won the huge total of 53 caps. Lawrie Reilly, the Hibernian forward who was also in the Wembley side of 1949, was another mainstay of the Scotland team. He claimed six goals in seven appearances against England, the most celebrated coming when he scored with the last touch of the match to snatch a 2–2 draw in 1953.

To this day, it remains the mission of Scotland's best players to leave us with memories as well as victories.

Dave **Mackay**

Dave Mackay had a little trick in which he would drop a coin on to his foot and then flick it up so that it dropped perfectly into his breast pocket. As a manager, he was known to instil humility on the training ground by placing the ball on the edge of the penalty area and then chipping it against the crossbar. Few could complete the manoeuvre with his consistency. It was also Mackay who scored with a couple of 25-yarders against Norway in 1963, one with his right foot, the other with his left.

These anecdotes make Mackay sound like the sort of adroit and ethereal ball-player in which Scotland once specialized. In fact, he was more commonly thought of as a dreadnought midfielder. The barrel-chested Mackay combined technique with a readiness to drive a side on. He was a key member of an uncannily adept generation and by the time he left Hearts in 1959, he had already won every honour on the Scottish scene.

Two years later, he was in the side when Spurs became the first English club this century to do the Double. His total of 22 caps for Scotland appears small, but ill-fortune limited his chances in some seasons. He broke his leg in 1963 and fractured it again when beginning his comeback.

Dave MACKAY

Position: Midfielder
Born: November 14, 1934
Birthplace: Edinburgh
Height: 5ft 8in.
Weight: 11st. 6lb
Club record:
Heart of Midlothian, Tottenham Hotspur, Derby County, Swindon Town
International record:
22 caps, 4 goals
International debut:
vs. Spain, May 26, 1957 (Madrid, lost 1–4)

From the school of hard knocks

Mackay had a hardiness that developed when, as a youngster, he played for Newtongrange Star against teams from mining villages. He recovered from the broken leg, although some people observed

Dave Mackay heads clear against England at Wembley in 1959

that his limp vanished completely only when he was on the field.

When he was hampered by weight problems and could no longer play in midfield, Brian Clough signed him for Derby County, in 1968, and asked Mackay to become a centre-half. He captained the side that won England's old Second Division. Promotion restored him to the top flight and in 1969, aged 34, Mackay shared the Footballer of the Year award with Tony Book.

He had played in the 1958 World Cup finals, but his best days coincided with Scotland's exasperating inability to return to that stage. Even so, his commitment was beyond question.

He played for the English Football League side that beat the Scottish League 1–0 in 1960 and confessed long afterwards that it was the only victory he had not enjoyed.

Jim **Baxter**

There have been too few opportunities for Scots to quibble over the precise manner in which England are beaten at Wembley, but Jim Baxter gave rise to one such debate. Footage of the 3–2 victory in 1967 is still shown, and in it the midfielder is to be seen playing keepy-uppy as he dawdles forward to flick a pass on to the chest of Denis Law.

The romantics love that cameo of disdain. The pragmatists think it would have been better if Baxter had just helped Scotland to score several more goals.

Although the opportunity to trounce England was missed that afternoon, it was in the player's nature to indulge his own whims. That practice frequently ensured success and immense entertainment was guaranteed. He possessed an innate skill that ensures he is numbered among the very greatest players this country has produced.

Jim BAXTER

Position: Midfielder
Born: September 29, 1939
Birthplace:
 Hill of Beath, Fife
Height: 5ft 10in.
Weight: 10st. 6lb
Club record:
 Raith Rovers, Rangers, Sunderland, Nottingham Forest, Rangers
International record:
 34 caps, 3 goals
International debut:
 vs. Northern Ireland, November 9, 1960 (Hampden, won 5–2)

"If he had applied himself," said former England manager Bobby Robson, "there might not have been a better player in the whole wide world." The reservations in Robson's statement reflect the poignancy that surrounds Baxter's story.

A wasted talent

Baxter was wayward, self-indulgent and almost allergic to hard work. When supporters fume over the failure of a magnificent bunch of players to realize their potential in World Cup football during the 1960s, it is always Baxter who is cited as the first example. The criticism is fair enough, and it is almost a tragic waste that he was finished in football when he was 30. All the same, Baxter and his peers were unlucky, too, that they were thwarted in the attempt to reach the 1962

A rare header from Jim Baxter, who had total control of England in 1967

World Cup by Czechoslovakia, the eventual runners-up to Brazil.

The midfielder must be appreciated in the context of his times. In his stylish arrogance, he presided over Rangers' domination of domestic football. During that decade, too, the annual match with England was still of overwhelming consequence and Baxter generally excelled in it.

The greatest expression of his superiority may have come in the 2–1 victory at Wembley in 1963, when he scored both of Scotland's goals. The second came from the penalty spot. Dave Mackay, the captain, had thrown the ball to him because, that day, the idea of Baxter missing was absurd.

He continues to face the charge that he squandered his genius. Baxter may care to reply that he was on the winning side in four of his five games with England.

Denis **Law**

Denis Law's reactions and awareness in the goalmouth intimidated defenders at Wembley in 1963

The raw material was not promising. The youngster who came to sign for Huddersfield Town as a 15-year-old was puny and wore thick glasses.

But Denis Law went on to become one of the most glamorous figures of the 1960s, exuding a panache that saw him termed "The King" by Manchester United fans at a time when Bobby Charlton and George Best were also at the club. There was a magnetism about Law that attracted as much attention as the quantity of his goals.

Law had been bought by Torino when he was only 21 but he loathed the sterile caution of Italian football and made his move to Old Trafford a year later. Dissatisfaction with Serie A was probably inevitable because, for him, the sport was founded on instinct and adventure.

Law had a heightened, intuitive sense of where the next chance might fall and he took those opportunities

---

Denis LAW

Position: Forward
Born: February 24, 1940
Birthplace: Aberdeen
Height: 5ft 9in.
Weight: 10st. 11lb
Club record:
   Huddersfield Town,
   Manchester City, Torino,
   Manchester United,
   Manchester City
International record:
   55 caps, 30 goals
International debut:
   vs. Wales, October 18,
   1958 (Cardiff, won 3–0)

---

with style. He understood the mood of the times, being one of the first to signify rebellion by wearing his jersey outside his shorts.

Despite the care in tending his image, there was nothing superficial about Law. Defenders discovered his raw desire for victory and Law was as quick as any centre-half to resort to the physical approach. Although injury prevented him from appearing in the 1968 European Cup final, when Manchester United overcame Benfica, the continent knew all about him. In 1964, Law was named European Footballer of the Year, and he remains the only Scot to have been so honoured.

Record holder

He and Kenny Dalglish share the record of 30 goals for Scotland and Law, the specialist finisher, reached the total in only 55 appearances. The forward was the youngest player this century to play for Scotland and the 18-year-old scored on his debut. He further endeared himself to Scots by preferring to play golf rather than watch England win the 1966 World Cup Final.

He claimed one of the goals in the 3–2 win at Wembley a year later. That afternoon was Scotland's greatest triumph of the decade, but Law was still playing when his country looked beyond the rivalries of these islands.

He made one appearance, against Zaire, in the 1974 World Cup finals and had played his part in the qualifier that eased Scotland through to that tournament. Recalled to the colours for the 1973 match with Czechoslovakia, Law did not score in the 2–1 win, but, at 33, produced a ceaseless endeavour that set the tone of an overwhelming evening.

Billy **Bremner**

In common with the majority of his countrymen, Billy Bremner wanted to see Scotland play England at Wembley during Euro 96. When it came to getting a ticket, he was in a privileged situation and needed only to make a phone call to join the VIPs, but he preferred to go to greater lengths to wangle a seat among the fans.

Bremner was even to be seen waving a flag at half-time in the match. His passion for Scotland had never really been forgotten, however, even if the scene came as an agreeable reminder.

His patriotism had been just as evident at the same ground in 1967, when his work on the pitch itself brought an even higher profile. Scotland beat England 3–2 that day, the first defeat Sir Alf Ramsey's team had endured since winning the World Cup the year before. "We're the world champions now," Bremner said.

The logic might have been faulty, but he had encapsulated the feeling of the supporters. Some might say that the red hair, combustible temper and penchant for getting into trouble made him an identikit Scot.

Distinctive footballer

His quality as a footballer, though, made him utterly distinctive. He and Johnny Giles formed a partnership of the highest calibre in the outstanding Leeds United team of the Don Revie era. Bremner was more fortunate than many of his gifted contemporaries who never found their proper stage in international football.

He survived to captain Scotland at the 1974 World Cup and looked as impressive a midfield player as any to be seen in the tournament. In the 0–0 draw with Brazil, the ball deflected against him and ran narrowly wide of the post, but, famous though the episode has become, it was barely a chance at all.

The performances in West Germany that summer allowed the rest of the world to acknowledge a player whose attributes had long been acclaimed by his fellow Scots. In England, recognition came not only

Bremner's inspiring leadership saw Scotland beat Czechoslovakia and qualify for the 1974 World Cup

through trophies gained with Leeds but also in the accolade of the Footballer of the Year award in 1970.

The combativeness that made him effective also created the occasional furore and an incident in Denmark in 1975 brought the end of his international career. By then, Bremner had already made sure of his place in the pantheon of Scottish football.

The depth of emotion when he died last year reflected the lasting impression he had made.

Billy BREMNER

Position: Midfielder
Born: December 9, 1942
Died: December 7, 1997
Birthplace: Stirling
Height: 5ft 5½ in.
Weight: 9st. 13lb
Club record:
  Leeds United, Hull City
International record:
  54 caps, 3 goals
International debut:
  vs. Spain, May 8, 1965
  (Hampden, drew 0–0)

Archie **Gemmill**

It took only a few seconds for Archie Gemmill to turn himself into an icon.

His second goal against Holland in the 3–2 victory at the 1978 World Cup summed up everything that Scots would like to believe about themselves. Here was a small and not especially photogenic man who might easily have been disregarded until the moment when his grit and individualistic impudence toppled celebrated opponents. In truth, Scottish football has rarely been like that, but Gemmill made it so for those moments in Argentina.

Oddly enough, that kind of intervention was not typical of his style. Three different managers made him captain of the national team, but none of them ever expected the midfielder to go dribbling through a gaggle of defenders.

Usually, it was his abundant vitality and an indefatigable nature that marked him out. It was typical of his stamina that he should last 20 years in British football. When everyone else was tiring, he could be counted upon to pitch his 5ft 5in. frame into a ball-winning tackle and then pick himself up to instigate another attack.

Despite his lack of height Archie Gemmill was a furious competitor for his country

---

Archie GEMMILL

Position: Midfielder
Born: March 24, 1947
Birthplace: Paisley
Height: 5ft 5in.
Weight: 11st. 2lb
Club record:
   St Mirren, Preston North End, Derby County, Nottingham Forest, Birmingham City, Jacksonville Teamen, Wigan Athletic, Derby County
International record:
   43 caps, 8 goals
International debut:
   vs. Belgium, February 3, 1971 (Liège, lost 0–3)

Proving himself

From the beginning he had been forced to prove himself and that experience may have nurtured his combativeness. Gemmill was with St Mirren and Preston North End, before he acquired the comparative prominence that came with a move to Derby County. There were ordeals to be faced with Scotland and, for some reason, he seemed to be punished with particular severity for a 1–0 defeat by England in 1972. A lesser person would have been disenchanted. More than three years were to pass before he was awarded his next cap, against Denmark in 1975.

The fact that he eventually made 43 appearances for Scotland over a span of 10 years was a sign of his disinclination ever to be brushed aside. He won two League Championship medals with Derby County and another with Nottingham Forest, where he was later to coach. The family service to the national team has continued in the form of his son Scot, who appeared in the qualifiers for the 1998 World Cup.

For all his durability, Gemmill senior has earned lasting fame for a single great contribution to the history of the World Cup. His jewel-like goal in Mendoza still gleams across 20 years.

Danny **McGrain**

Danny McGrain never seemed to have niggling injuries, but while he remained free of groin strains and pulled hamstrings the defender was prone to grave medical problems. He suffered a fractured skull in 1972, found he was diabetic after the 1974 World Cup and missed the 1978 tournament during a long period in which a chronic ankle injury kept him out of football.

Danny McGRAIN	
Position: Full-back	
Born: May 1, 1950	
Birthplace: Glasgow	
Height: 5ft 9in.	
Weight: 12st. 1lb	
Club record: Celtic	
International record: 62 caps, 0 goals	
International debut: vs. Wales, May 12, 1973 (Wrexham, won 2–0)	

Overcoming those difficulties would have been a great accomplishment for anyone, but McGrain also went on to prove himself one of the greatest of full-backs. In the seasons immediately following his fractured skull, Scots were prone to argue that McGrain was the finest right-back in the world. It was a tenable argument, for his range of skills was almost complete.

McGrain might have been seized by uncertainty when the occasional chance to score presented itself, but he overlapped with verve and was the best winger as well as the best defender in many of the matches he played.

His tackling too had a sense of adventure. Fullbacks are often taught to stay on their feet and back away from forwards until the right moment to challenge presents itself. In his heyday, McGrain's timing of the tackle justified him in ignoring such advice. He loved to pounce in, win the ball and assume control of the situation.

A team player

At the 1974 World Cup, McGrain sacrificed some of his potential by playing at left-back so that the splendid Sandy Jardine could be accommodated on the right. His value to Scotland was rarely concealed wherever he happened to be standing.

Much was made of his knack for dominating the admired Welsh winger Leighton James, but no jinx was involved. McGrain was too good for most opponents. Scotland missed him terribly at the 1978 World Cup and he did not return to the national team until 1979. The injury had diminished his physical condition, but he still won 22 caps after he returned to international action.

If his gusto and buccaneering runs were no longer possible, McGrain compensated with know-how and force of character. Jock Stein made him Scotland's captain for the first time for a friendly match in Poland in 1980. He held the position in the build-up to the 1982 World Cup and led out the team for the opening match of the tournament, against New Zealand. Given the ordeals that he endured, it was remarkable that McGrain could prove so important a player throughout so long a career.

At his peak Danny McGrain was one of the best full-backs in the world

Kenny **Dalglish**

Kenny Dalglish is probably the greatest footballer Scotland has ever produced.

In addition to imagination and skill, he possessed a dedication that had been all too rare among many of his wonderfully entertaining predecessors. Dalglish was never to be parted from his single-mindedness.

> **Kenny DALGLISH**
>
> **Position:** Forward
> **Born:** March 4, 1951
> **Birthplace:** Glasgow
> **Height:** 5ft 8in.
> **Weight:** 11st. 13lb
> **Club record:**
>   Celtic, Liverpool
> **International record:**
>   102 caps, 30 goals
> **International debut:**
>   vs. Belgium, November 10,
>   1971 (Pittodrie, won 1–0)

Many of his goals were a delight to witness, but he did not set out to amuse himself. The forward was always intent on victory and knew exactly what was required to achieve it.

There was no eccentricity, although he was capable of great individual goals and was at his most flamboyant in a Celtic side that depended on him. The mature Dalglish had adjusted his style to ensure the maximum benefit to the teams he played for. Lacking pace, he became adept at playing with his back to goal and using an acute knowledge of the shifting geometry of a match to release others into space. At Liverpool, the prolific Ian Rush was the main beneficiary.

Most capped player

Although delicate of touch, Dalglish was physically sturdy and rarely missed a match. He won the European Cup three times with Liverpool and his longevity took him to the record total of 102 caps. He was around long enough to see his reputation fluctuate.

Despite a winning goal against England in 1976 that was driven through the legs of Ray Clemence, Dalglish, in the early days, had to endure expressions of disappointment from people who felt he ought always to be capable of single-handedly ensuring victory. Latterly, however, he was fully appreciated.

A great player in a struggling team, but Kenny Dalglish's commitment to Scotland did not falter

Dalglish equalled Denis Law's record for Scotland of 30 goals, but creating chances was as much his *forte* as taking them. His first World Cup finals appearance came in 1974 and only injury kept him out of the tournament in Mexico 12 years later.

Few people have been able to prosper at so high a level for so long a period. As a manager with Liverpool, Blackburn Rovers and Newcastle United, he has become known for his guarded responses and sardonic sense of humour, but a deep passion for the game has always been evident.

After he had turned inside from the right wing to flight a beautiful and important goal against Spain in a World Cup qualifier in 1984, the cameras caught his reaction. He was then 33, but it was as if the ecstasy had wiped a dozen years from his face.

Joe **Jordan**

The swaying, crammed terracing of the old Hampden Park was a great place to capture the excitement of a game, but a very poor vantage point to take in the detail. Thus it took a while to find out that it was substitute Joe Jordan who had headed the winner against Czechoslovakia in 1973.

This goal, and 2–1 victory, took Scotland to the World Cup finals for the first time since 1958. Once the centre-forward's identity was verified everything changed for Jordan. Instead of being a young fringe player at Leeds United, he became a champion of Scotland's cause.

Despite moves to Manchester United and AC Milan, the crescendos came with his country. His power and unflinching style looked suited to wars of attrition, but he had a wonderful habit of putting his occasional goals to the most precious use. His 11 goals for Scotland included efforts that were crucial to qualification for the World Cup finals of 1974, but also of 1978 and 1982. He found the net at each of those tournaments.

Making them count

Jordan did not forget to deal with England either, supplying the first in a 2–0 win at Hampden in 1974. Some searching is required before you discover a goal of his that did not possess consequence. There was only one.

Why did he bother to punish Norway in a friendly? The forward also made sure of his place in folklore by being involved in the obscure events that led to Scotland receiving a vital penalty against Wales at Anfield in the 1977 qualifier.

Joe Jordan relishes his goal against Russia. The World Cup brought out the best in him

He was a talisman long before then, in any case. The image of Jordan with his teeth out had been the key image in an advertising campaign for a brand of lager. Somehow the line of bare gum only hinted at bite. Supporters appreciated him because they knew what a trial Jordan could be to any defence.

He spared himself nothing, which may explain why he also had to cope with many injuries. Jordan's greatest strength lay in single-mindedness rather than muscle. It was evident in his final goal for Scotland.

He and Steve Archibald both had the chance to fasten on to a loose ball, but Jordan did not risk any misunderstanding and decisively took control of the situation to put Scotland 1–0 ahead of the USSR in the eventual 2–2 draw at the 1978 World Cup. Deferring to Jordan was usually a prudent policy.

Joe JORDAN

Position: Forward
Born: December 15, 1951
Birthplace: Carluke
Height: 6ft
Weight: 11st. 12lb
Club record:
Morton, Leeds United, Manchester United, AC Milan, Verona, Southampton, Bristol City
International record:
52 caps, 11 goals
International debut:
vs. England, May 19, 1973 (Wembley, lost 0–1)

Graeme **Souness**

Graeme Souness found himself embroiled in several controversies, but he was never hampered by a crisis of confidence when he set out to resolve them. Even as a youngster he had walked out of Tottenham Hotspur because they would not grant him an immediate place in the first team.

Wilfulness might have been harmful to him but, at Middlesbrough, he had Jack Charlton as manager and the veteran Scotland midfielder Bobby Murdoch to apply guidance. He could still be provocative, and sometimes seemed to relish the occasional inflammatory deed, but he did mature into an imperious and extremely tough midfielder in a masterful Liverpool team.

The last of his three European Cup winners' medals was seized, in 1984, against AS Roma in Rome. Liverpool defeated the Italians in a shoot-out and, amid the bedlam of the home support, the manner in which Souness briskly slammed his penalty into the top corner was disdainful.

The strength of his spirit was appreciated by the Scotland manager Jock Stein and the midfielder was his captain. Life could never be as smooth with his country as it was with his all-conquering club, but Souness's sharp, scrupulous passing was the perfect instrument for international football. Where Scotland were concerned, the classic illustration of his style probably came in a friendly, when Yugoslavia were beaten 6–1 at Hampden in 1984.

Left too late

Circumstances were often unhelpful to him and any constraints imposed on Souness were to the great detriment of Scotland's hopes. He was 25 at the time of the 1978 World Cup in Argentina and surely ready to impress.

Graeme SOUNESS	
Position: Midfielder	
Born: May 6, 1953	
Birthplace: Edinburgh	
Height: 5ft 11in.	
Weight: 12st. 13lb	
Club record:	
Tottenham Hotspur, Middlesbrough, Liverpool, Sampdoria, Rangers	
International record:	
54 caps, 4 goals	
International debut:	
vs. East Germany, October 30, 1974 (Hampden, won 3–0)	

Ally MacLeod, however, kept faith with an ageing partnership of Bruce Rioch and Don Masson in midfield for a 3–1 defeat by Peru and a 1–1 draw with Iran. Souness was introduced only for the last match and made himself utterly at home in the celebrated victory over Holland.

By the time of the 1986 World Cup, he was to discover for himself how hard it can be for a veteran to prosper in the exhausting South American climate. His real chance had come four years earlier in Spain. Despite his expertly placed equalizer against the USSR, Scotland failed on goal difference to qualify for the second stage of the 1982 tournament.

In his travels as player and manager, however, Souness has shown that a Scot can take his place among the cosmopolitan figures of the game.

Graeme Souness ensured that respect for the Scottish footballer did not fade

Alex **McLeish**

Alex McLEISH
Position: Centre-half
Born: January 21, 1959
Birthplace: Glasgow
Height: 6ft 1in.
Weight: 12st. 4lb
Club record:
Aberdeen, Motherwell
International record:
77 caps, 0 goals
International debut:
vs. Portugal,
March 26, 1980
(Hampden, won 4–1)

There is something in the Scottish character that shuns security, and fans rarely seem to reminisce over central defenders of yesteryear, but an exception will always be made for the Aberdeen pairing of Alex McLeish and Willie Miller.

In a triumvirate formed with the goalkeeper Jim Leighton, they provided a marvellous defensive foundation that allowed the construction of a triumph when Aberdeen won the Cup-Winners' Cup in 1983. He and Miller dovetailed perfectly, with McLeish often making the initial challenge and his partner guaranteeing the close marking that nullified any subsequent threat.

There were many opportunities to admire McLeish. His longevity as a footballer saw him represent Scotland over a period of 13 years and his total of 77 caps is inferior only to those of Leighton and Kenny Dalglish. The nature of the Scotland team meant that McLeish and Miller did not always get the chance to work in tandem at international level.

Various managers had to select sides that also contained other expert defenders of the period such as Paul Hegarty, David Narey and Alan Hansen. McLeish won his first cap as an anchorman in midfield and he would return to that role on other occasions.

Beating the Old Enemy

Despite that, there was one high-profile match in which McLeish and Miller were able to show a wide audience where their real accomplishment lay. They were chosen as the centre-backs against England at Wembley in 1981.

Commentators south of the border were politely sceptical about the preference for two men from the Scottish League in such key positions. The game itself was a tedious affair, but the dullness was a conse-

Alex McLeish's decisiveness when leaping for the ball was at the heart of sound Scottish defending

quence of the effectiveness of Miller and McLeish in denying England opportunities. John Robertson's successful penalty kick for Scotland proved to be the only goal but, that day, McLeish ensured that it was no longer possible for anyone in British football to underestimate his worth.

A centre-half ought to be built to last and McLeish gradually prospered at international level. Jock Stein used him as a substitute against Brazil in the 1982 World Cup. Four years later, he was unwell in the Mexico tournament and Alex Ferguson, his then manager at Aberdeen, could only select him for the first match, against Denmark. In the 1990 World Cup, Andy Roxburgh picked him for all three matches.

As that record of perseverance indicates, McLeish was a very hard defender to shake off.

Chapter 7
World Cup Records

Scotland's qualification for the 1998 World Cup in France continues their remarkably consistent record in the tournament. Since their first appearance in 1954, Scotland have made it to eight of the last 12 finals.

BRAZIL 1950

WORLD CUP QUALIFIERS

Date	Opponents	Venue	Score
1.10.49	Northern Ireland	Belfast	8–2
9.11.49	Wales	Hampden	2–0
15.4.50	England	Hampden	0–1

1950 Table	P	W	D	L	F	A	Pts
England	3	3	0	0	14	3	6
Scotland	3	2	0	1	10	3	4
Wales	3	0	1	2	1	6	1
Northern Ireland	3	0	1	2	4	17	1

Scotland qualified but declined to compete

SWITZERLAND 1954

WORLD CUP QUALIFIERS

Date	Opponents	Venue	Score
3.10.53	Northern Ireland	Belfast	3–1
4.11.53	Wales	Hampden	3–3
3.4.54	England	Hampden	2–4

1954 Table	P	W	D	L	F	A	Pts
England	3	3	0	0	11	4	6
Scotland	3	1	1	1	8	8	3
Northern Ireland	3	1	0	2	4	7	2
Wales	3	0	1	2	5	9	1

WORLD CUP FINALS

Date	Opponents	Venue	Score
16.6.54	Austria	Zurich	0–1
19.6.54	Uruguay	Basle	0–7

Final Pool 3 Table	P	W	D	L	F	A	Pts
Uruguay	2	2	0	0	9	0	4
Austria	2	2	0	0	6	0	4
Czechoslovakia	2	0	0	2	0	7	0
Scotland	2	0	0	2	0	8	0

Billy Liddell for Scotland and Alf Ramsey for England in 1953

SWEDEN 1958

WORLD CUP QUALIFIERS

Date	Opponents	Venue	Score
8.5.57	Spain	Hampden	4–2
19.5.57	Switzerland	Basle	2–1
26.5.57	Spain	Madrid	1–4
6.11.57	Switzerland	Hampden	3–2

1958 Table	P	W	D	L	F	A	Pts
Scotland	4	3	0	1	10	9	6
Spain	4	2	1	1	12	8	5
Switzerland	4	0	1	3	6	11	1

WORLD CUP FINALS

Date	Opponents	Venue	Score
8.6.58	Yugoslavia	Vasteras	1–1
11.6.58	Paraguay	Norrköping	2–3
15.6.58	France	Örebro	1–2

Final Pool 2 Table	P	W	D	L	F	A	Pts
France	3	2	0	1	11	7	4
Yugoslavia	3	1	2	0	7	6	4
Paraguay	3	1	1	1	9	12	3
Scotland	3	0	1	2	4	6	1

CHILE 1962

WORLD CUP QUALIFIERS

Date	Opponents	Venue	Score
3.5.61	Rep. of Ireland	Hampden	4–1
7.5.61	Rep. of Ireland	Dublin	3–0
14.5.61	Czechoslovakia	Bratislava	0–4
26.9.61	Czechoslovakia	Hampden	3–2
29.11.61	Czechoslovakia	Brussels*	2–4

1962 Table	P	W	D	L	F	A	Pts
Czechoslovakia	4	3	0	1	16	5	6
Scotland	4	3	0	1	10	7	6
Rep. of Ireland	4	0	0	4	3	17	0

Scotland failed to qualify   *play-off

ENGLAND 1966

WORLD CUP QUALIFIERS

Date	Opponents	Venue	Score
21.10.64	Finland	Hampden	3–1
23.5.65	Poland	Chorzow	1–1
27.5.65	Finland	Helsinki	2–1
13.10.65	Poland	Hampden	1–2
9.11.65	Italy	Hampden	1–0
7.12.65	Italy	Naples	0–3

1966 Table	P	W	D	L	F	A	Pts
Italy	6	4	1	1	17	3	9
Scotland	6	3	1	2	8	8	7
Poland	6	2	2	2	11	10	6
Finland	6	1	0	5	5	20	2

Scotland failed to qualify

MEXICO 1970

WORLD CUP QUALIFIERS

Date	Opponents	Venue	Score
6.11.68	Austria	Hampden	2–1
11.12.68	Cyprus	Nicosia	5–0
16.4.69	West Germany	Hampden	1–1
17.5.69	Cyprus	Hampden	8–0
22.10.69	West Germany	Hamburg	2–3
5.11.69	Austria	Vienna	0–2

1970 Table	P	W	D	L	F	A	Pts
West Germany	6	5	1	0	20	3	11
Scotland	6	3	1	2	18	7	7
Austria	6	3	0	3	12	7	6
Cyprus	6	0	0	6	2	35	0

Scotland failed to qualify

Billy Bremner makes his way through the Yugoslavian team in Scotland's World Cup game from 1974. The full time score was 1–1 – and Yugoslavia went through on goal difference

WEST GERMANY 1974

WORLD CUP QUALIFIERS

Date	Opponents	Venue	Score
18.10.72	Denmark	Copenhagen	4–1
15.11.72	Denmark	Hampden	2–0
26.9.73	Czechoslovakia	Hampden	2–1
17.10.73	Czechoslovakia	Bratislava	0–1

1974 Table	P	W	D	L	F	A	Pts
Scotland	4	3	0	1	8	3	6
Czechoslovakia	4	2	1	1	9	3	5
Denmark	4	0	1	3	2	13	1

WORLD CUP FINALS

Date	Opponents	Venue	Score
14.6.74	Zaire	Dortmund	0–2
18.6.74	Brazil	Frankfurt	0–0
22.6.74	Yugoslavia	Frankfurt	1–1

Final Group 2 Table	P	W	D	L	F	A	Pts
Yugoslavia	3	1	2	0	10	1	4
Brazil	3	1	2	0	3	0	4
Scotland	3	1	2	0	3	1	4
Zaire	3	0	0	3	0	14	0

ARGENTINA 1978

WORLD CUP QUALIFIERS

Date	Opponents	Venue	Score
13.10.76	Czechoslovakia	Prague	0–2
17.11.76	Wales	Hampden	1–0
21.9.77	Czechoslovakia	Hampden	3–1
12.10.77	Wales	Liverpool	2–0

1978 Table	P	W	D	L	F	A	Pts
Scotland	4	3	0	1	6	3	6
Czechoslovakia	4	2	0	2	4	6	4
Wales	4	1	0	3	3	4	2

WORLD CUP FINALS

Date	Opponents	Venue	Score
3.6.78	Peru	Cordoba	1–3
7.6.78	Iran	Cordoba	1–1
11.6.78	Holland	Mendoza	3–2

Final Group 4 Table	P	W	D	L	F	A	Pts
Peru	3	2	1	0	7	2	5
Holland	3	1	1	1	5	3	3
Scotland	3	1	1	1	5	6	3
Iran	3	0	1	2	2	8	1

SPAIN 1982

WORLD CUP QUALIFIERS

Date	Opponents	Venue	Score
10.9.80	Sweden	Stockholm	1–0
15.10.80	Portugal	Hampden	0–0
25.2.81	Israel	Tel Aviv	1–0
25.3.81	Northern Ireland	Hampden	1–1
28.4.81	Israel	Hampden	3–1
9.9.81	Sweden	Hampden	2–0
14.10.81	Northern Ireland	Belfast	0–0
18.11.81	Portugal	Lisbon	1–2

1982 Table	P	W	D	L	F	A	Pts
Scotland	8	4	3	1	9	4	11
Northern Ireland	8	3	3	2	6	3	9
Sweden	8	3	2	3	7	8	8
Portugal	8	3	1	4	8	11	7
Israel	8	1	3	4	6	10	5

WORLD CUP FINALS

Date	Opponents	Venue	Score
15.6.82	New Zealand	Malaga	5–2
18.6.82	Brazil	Seville	1–4
22.6.82	USSR	Malaga	2–2

Final Group 6 Table	P	W	D	L	F	A	Pts
Brazil	3	3	0	0	10	2	6
Soviet Union	3	1	1	1	6	4	3
Scotland	3	1	1	1	8	8	3
New Zealand	3	0	0	3	2	12	0

**Joe Jordan scores against Israel in 1981.
Scotland qualified for the 1982 World Cup
Finals by topping their group**

MEXICO 1986

WORLD CUP QUALIFIERS

Date	Opponents	Venue	Score
17.10.84	Iceland	Hampden	3–0
14.11.84	Spain	Hampden	3–1
27.2.85	Spain	Seville	0–1
27.3.85	Wales	Hampden	0–1
28.5.85	Iceland	Reykjavik	1–0
10.9.85	Wales	Cardiff	1–1
20.11.85*	Australia	Hampden	2–0
4.12.85*	Australia	Melbourne	0–0

1986 Table	P	W	D	L	F	A	Pts
Spain	6	4	0	2	9	8	8
Scotland	6	3	1	2	8	4	7
Wales	6	3	1	2	7	6	7
Iceland	6	1	0	5	4	10	2

WORLD CUP FINALS

Date	Opponents	Venue	Score
4.6.86	Denmark	Nezahualcoyot	0–1
8.6.86	West Germany	Queretaro	1–2
13.6.86	Uruguay	Nezahualcoyot	0–0

Final Group E Table	P	W	D	L	F	A	Pts
Denmark	3	3	0	0	9	1	6
West Germany	3	1	1	1	3	4	3
Uruguay	3	0	2	1	2	7	2
Scotland	3	0	1	2	1	3	1

*play-off

ITALY 1990

WORLD CUP QUALIFIERS

Date	Opponents	Venue	Score
14.9.88	Norway	Oslo	2–1
19.10.88	Yugoslavia	Hampden	1–1
8.2.89	Cyprus	Limassol	3–2
8.3.89	France	Hampden	2–0
26.4.89	Cyprus	Hampden	2–1
6.9.89	Yugoslavia	Zagreb	1–3
11.10.89	France	Paris	0–3
15.11.89	Norway	Hampden	1–1

1990 Table	P	W	D	L	F	A	Pts
Yugoslavia	8	6	2	0	16	6	14
Scotland	8	4	2	2	12	12	10
France	8	3	3	2	10	7	9
Norway	8	2	2	4	10	9	6
Cyprus	8	0	1	7	6	20	1

WORLD CUP FINALS

Date	Opponents	Venue	Score
11.6.90	Costa Rica	Genoa	0–1
16.6.90	Sweden	Genoa	2–1
20.6.90	Brazil	Turin	0–1

Final Group C Table	P	W	D	L	F	A	Pts
Brazil	3	3	0	0	4	1	6
Costa Rica	3	2	0	1	3	2	4
Scotland	3	1	0	2	2	3	2
Sweden	3	0	0	3	3	6	0

USA 1994

WORLD CUP QUALIFIERS

Date	Opponents	Venue	Score
9.9.92	Switzerland	Berne	1–3
14.10.92	Portugal	Ibrox	0–0
18.11.92	Italy	Ibrox	0–0
17.2.93	Malta	Ibrox	3–0
28.4.93	Portugal	Lisbon	0–5
19.5.93	Estonia	Tallinn	3–0
2.6.93	Estonia	Aberdeen	3–1
8.9.93	Switzerland	Aberdeen	1–1
13.10.93	Italy	Rome	1–3
17.11.93	Malta	Valletta	2–0

1994 Table	P	W	D	L	F	A	Pts
Italy	10	7	2	1	22	7	16
Switzerland	10	6	3	1	23	6	15
Portugal	10	6	2	2	18	5	14
Scotland	10	4	3	3	14	13	11
Malta	10	1	1	8	3	23	3
Estonia	10	0	1	9	1	27	1

FRANCE 1998

WORLD CUP QUALIFIERS

Date	Opponents	Venue	Score
31.8.96	Austria	Vienna	0–0
5.10.96	Latvia	Riga	2–0
9.10.96	Estonia	Tallinn	Abandoned
10.11.96	Sweden	Ibrox	1–0
11.2.97	Estonia	Monaco	0–0
29.3.97	Estonia	Kilmarnock	2–0
2.4.97	Austria	Celtic Park	2–0
30.4.97	Sweden	Gothenburg	1–2
8.6.97	Belarus	Minsk	1–0
7.9.97	Belarus	Aberdeen	4–1
11.10.97	Latvia	Celtic Park	2–0

1998 Table	P	W	D	L	F	A	Pts
Austria	10	8	1	1	17	4	25
Scotland	10	7	2	1	15	3	23
Sweden	10	7	0	3	16	9	21
Latvia	10	3	1	6	10	14	10
Estonia	10	1	1	8	4	16	4
Belarus	10	1	1	8	5	21	4

COMPLETE WORLD CUP RECORD 1949–1997

	P	W	D	L	F	A
Finals	20	4	6	10	23	35
Qualifiers	79	44	15	20	140	88
Overall	99	48	21	30	163	123

Index

Acknowledgements

The publishers would like to thank the following sources for their kind permission to reproduce the pictures in this book:

Allsport UK Ltd 94, 95/Keith Beckley 27; Shaun Botterill 10, 70; Clive Brunskill 8, 12, 18, 30, 64, 67, 69; David Cannon 105; Phil Cole 62; Stu Forster 44; Mike Hewitt 68; Ross Kinnaird 53; Ben Radford 4b, 14, 16, 21, 22, 23, 50, 92; Mark Thompson 46; Vandystadt 15. Colorsport 4t, 11, 17, 24, 39, 40, 47, 48, 49, 51, 52, 54, 63, 72, 76, 81, 84, 86, 88, 89, 90, 93, 96, 98, 99, 100, 102, 104, 106, 107, 108. Empics/Mathew Ashton 33, 66. Hulton Getty 80. Mark Leech 5, 6, 45, 65. Popperfoto 9, 13, 19, 34, 77, 79, 82, 83, 91, 97/Dave Joiner 60; Reuters 20, 28, 55, 57, 61. Scottish News & Sport 29, 31, 35, 37, 74, 42/Jeff Holmes 26,32,38; Alan Harvey 41. Sporting Pictures (UK) Ltd 25, 56, 58, 59, 71, 87, 101, 103.

Every effort has been made to acknowledge correctly and contact the source and/or copyright holder of each picture, and Carlton Books Limited apologises for any unintentional errors or omissions which will be corrected in future editions of this book.